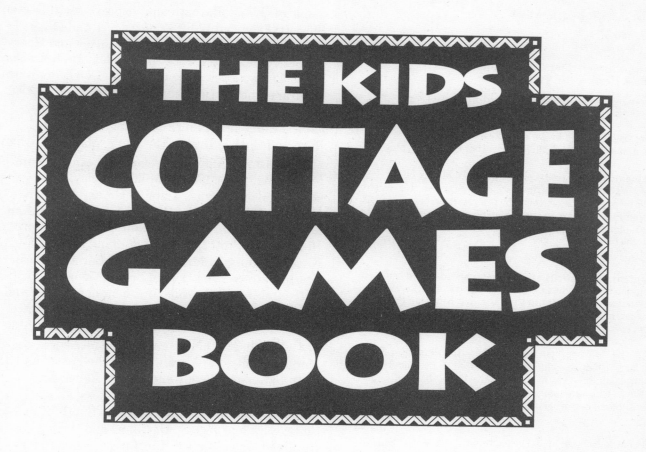

THE KIDS COTTAGE GAMES BOOK

BY JANE DRAKE & ANN LOVE

ILLUSTRATED BY HEATHER COLLINS

KIDS CAN PRESS

Canadian Cataloguing in Publication Data

Drake, Jane
    The kids cottage games book

Includes index.
ISBN 1-55074-467-4

1. Games – Juvenile literature. I. Love, Ann.
II. Collins, Heather. III. Title.

GV1203.D73 1998   j790.1'922   C97-931619-7

We acknowledge with appreciation the support of the Canada Council for the Arts and the Ontario Arts Council for our publishing program.

Published in Canada by
Kids Can Press Ltd.
29 Birch Avenue
Toronto, ON M4V 1E2

Published in the U.S. by
Kids Can Press Ltd.
85 River Rock Drive, Suite 202
Buffalo, NY 14207

Series editor: Laurie Wark
Edited by Trudee Romanek
Designed by Blair Kerrigan/Glyphics
Printed and bound in Canada by Kromar Printing Limited

 Text stock contains over 50% recycled paper

CDN 98 0 9 8 7 6 5 4 3 2 1

ACKNOWLEDGMENTS

Sandra Ackland; Barbara and Victor Barnett; Doreen Barnett; Fran and Will Barnett; Joyce and Peter Barnett; Judy and Ian Barnett; Kathleen and Henry Barnett; Neil Beatty; Jack Brickenden; Trish Brooks; David Cayley; Becky Cheung; Nellie Chisholm; Barb Cochrane; the Corrigan family backyard; Jane Crist; Alan Downward; Paula Draimin; Cindy, Patricia, James, Emily and Tom Drake; Marybeth Drake; Ruth and Charlie Drake; Stephanie, Madeline, Brian and Jim Drake; Mari Ellery; Gerald Feeney; Grant Gibson; Willie Goldbloom; Millie Gourlay; Bob Graham; Jennie Gruss; Camilla Gryski; Pat Hancock; Christine, Natalie and Doug Hedden; Anne MacDonald Hilmer; Robert Hunt; Julie Hunt-Correa; Heather and Scott Irwin; Dawn Khoury; Martha Kilgour Adams; Lynda King; David Latimer; Jackie Leech; Cathleen and Donald Leitch; Ganeil Liburd; Betty and Gage Love; Melanie, Jennifer, Adrian and David Love; Peter Love; Gar Mahood; the Manchee family; Rebecca Marshall; the McClure family; Kim McCullough; Mimi McEvenue; Jane McKenzie; the Morgan family; the Morley family; the Passi family; Lynn Patterson; Wendy and George Reifel; Erin Renaud; Michael Robson; Cynthia Ross; Michael Roth; the Sedgwick family; Florence Smith; Kim Spice; Barb and Jack Spitler; Jane and Doug Stewart; Ruth and Walt Stewart; Kim Tanaka; Dr. and Mrs. Tashiro; Mary Thompson; Derek Totten; Bonnie and Russell Usher; Elizabeth Vosburgh; Jennifer Ward; Debbie Wells; Dorothy and Herb Wyngard.

The authors gratefully acknowledge the continued support of Valerie Hussey, Ricky Englander and the enthusiastic staff at Kids Can Press. We enjoyed working with editor Trudee Romanek whose attention to detail fine-tuned the most complicated instructions. Heather Collins's illustrations and Blair Kerrigan's design work complete this trilogy beautifully.

This book is dedicated to our childhood friends,
with whom we learned
to win and lose, play fair, bluff, cheat
and have fun.

Jennifer Cayley, Jane Morley Cobden,
Marg Stockwell Hart, Wendy Corrigan McCreath,
Betsy Kofman Bascom, Gerri Draimin,
Penny McClure, Hilary Robinson,
Stephanie Smith

CONTENTS

INDOOR GAMES

GAMES TO MAKE

WATERFRONT

WARM WEATHER OLYMPICS

LAND ACTION

The screen door slams and you're
outdoors, raring to go. Gather up the gang
and choose from one of these active
summer games. There is something for
everyone, whether you're a family group
or a pack of kids the same age. This
section will give you the rules and tips for
familiar favorites as well as some new
outdoor games.

TIPS FOR CHOOSING TEAMS

Make dividing into teams as fair as possible by following these guidelines:

- Choose teams quickly so the fun can begin.

- If everyone is of similar ability, use cards or slips of paper to divide the group evenly. If there are eight people, put four spades and four hearts from a deck of cards in a cap. Each player picks a card and joins the appropriate team.

- When dividing a large group in which the players are of various ages and abilities, choose two captains. They each take turns choosing teammates with:

  brown eyes

  a ponytail

  the newest shoes

  no socks

  a missing or wiggly tooth

  pierced ear(s)

  braces

WHO GOES FIRST?

If you're tired of flipping coins, spinning rackets or picking a number, decide who goes first using a suggestion from this list:

The person whose birthday is closest to June 21 (New Year's Day, Groundhog Day)

The person who is farthest away from her home

The person with the most pets

The person with the most mosquito bites

The person with the craziest sunglasses

The person with the most scars

The person who can sing the highest note

The person who can sing the lowest note . . .

FOR THE RECORD

Start a record book and keep track of the games you play. Note the weekly hearts champion, record who did the funniest charade all summer, write down the date you took your friends to the cleaners in rumoli. If you spend the summer at the same place or with the same people year after year, keep the record book up to date. It is fun to look back and remember when Grandpa won at cheat or when your brother finally learned to shuffle cards and deal by himself.

SPUD

When the picnic is over and it's time to get moving, SPUD is the game of choice. All you need is a flat playing area, four or more players and a soft ball such as a tennis ball.

PLAYING THE GAME

Ask an adult to whisper a number in the ear of each player. With four players, use numbers 1 to 6; five players, numbers 1 to 7 and so on.

1.

Choose someone to be It.

2.

Gather within touching distance of It. She shouts out a number and throws the ball high in the air. If your number is called, you become It and chase the ball. Everyone else runs as far away as possible.

3.

When you've retrieved the ball, yell "SPUD!" All other players freeze. Take three giant steps toward the nearest player and try to hit this person with the ball. Frozen players are allowed to sway and duck to avoid being hit by the ball, but they are not allowed to move their feet.

4.

If you hit a player, that person has one penalty against him, or an S, and he becomes It. If you miss him, *you* get an S. You retrieve the ball, and throw it up and call another number as in step 2.

5.

You are out of the game once you have four penalties or SPUD.

6.

If you call a ghost number — a number not assigned to anyone or a number of a player who is out of the game — you have to chase the ball yourself.

500 UP

It's a perfect day for baseball but you don't have enough players for a game. Why not play 500 Up? You'll still get that warm, timeless, baseball feeling — and practice your skills at the same time. You'll need two or more players, a bat, a ball and baseball gloves if you have them and a large open area so you can hit the ball safely. If you don't have a baseball and bat, a tennis ball and racket will do.

PLAYING THE GAME

One player starts as the batter and everyone else is a fielder. The batter stands at one end of the field, throws the ball up in the air and hits it out into the field.

All fielders try to catch the ball. The fielder who does, scores a certain number of points depending on the type of catch. Any fielder who tries for the ball and fumbles it loses points. When a player tallies up 500 points, that player becomes the new batter and the previous batter takes a place in the field. The game goes on until you run out of energy.

SCORING

A fielder who catches	A fielder who fumbles and misses
a fly, earns 100 points	a fly, loses 100 points
a ball that bounces once, earns 75 points	a ball that bounces once, loses 75 points
a ball that bounces twice, earns 50 points	a ball that bounces twice, loses 50 points
a ball that bounces more than twice (a grounder), earns 25 points	a ball that bounces more than twice (a grounder), loses 25 points

THE DOG DAYS OF SUMMER

Major league baseball fans call late August, "the dog days of summer." The dog days bring long, hot afternoon games with teams struggling for playoff spots or hopelessly playing out the rest of the season.

In fact, the expression is far older than baseball. It began with a group of five bright stars ancient people thought looked like a dog. The dog constellation, or Canis Major, starts to rise just before dawn in August. Sirius, the dog's eye, is the brightest star in the sky, much brighter than the Sun — but farther away. Because Sirius is so bright, you can still see it after the sun rises and the rest of the stars have disappeared from view. Two thousand years ago in Rome, people knew that when Sirius appeared in the August morning sky, the dog days had arrived and the late summer heat would soon follow.

HORSESHOES

Horseshoes is an easygoing game for two to four players, good for a long, hot summer day. You'll need four horseshoes and two sturdy metal stakes about 60 cm (25 in.) long driven into two circular sand pits about 12 m (40 ft.) apart.

PLAYING THE GAME

Each player gets two horseshoes. In a game of singles, both players stand beside the stake in one of the sand pits.

1.

The first player tosses one horseshoe and then the other, trying to ring the opposite stake. The other players and spectators stand behind the person throwing.

2.

When the first player has thrown both horseshoes, it's the opponent's turn to throw.

3.

Then the players walk together to the other end and score the inning.

4.

Whoever has the highest score throws first in the next inning. If the score is tied, then the person who went second leads next time.

5.

The players toss the horseshoes back to the first stake. The game continues until one player reaches 50 points to win.

6.

For a four-player game, players divide into two teams. One person from each team stands at each stake. The two opponents at one stake each toss two horseshoes as in singles, and their scores are tallied. Then their teammates at the other stake throw the horseshoes back and their scores are added on. The first team to reach 50 points wins.

SCORING

- To count, a horseshoe must hit the ground inside the sand pit and stop within 15 cm (6 in.) of the target stake. Remove any horseshoe that bounces into the sand pit.

- A ringer, worth 3 points, is a horseshoe that circles the stake so that a straight line can be drawn from one prong to the other without touching the stake.

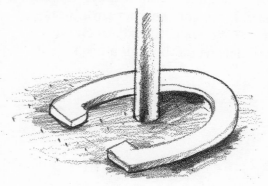

- Score 1 point for each nonringer that lands closer than an opponent's.

- Opposing horseshoes that are exactly the same distance from the stake cancel each other out.

TIPS FOR GOOD THROWING

1.
Grip the horseshoe with your fingers curling under the middle of the "u" or the middle of one of the arms. Experiment to see how each grip makes the shoe turn in the air.

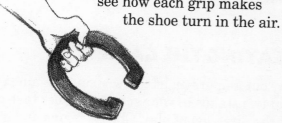

2.
As you toss, bend the knee that's on the same side as your throwing arm and step forward with your other leg.

3.
When the shoe swings up so it's in line with your eyes and the peg, let go. Don't hurl the horseshoe, let its weight do the work.

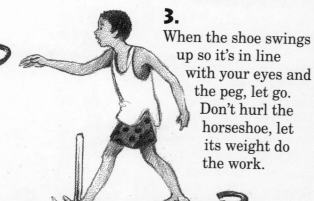

CROQUET

For a lively game of croquet, you'll need two teams of one to three players each, a well-cut lawn and a croquet set.

PLAYING THE GAME

Lay out a figure-eight course using the nine hoops and two stakes in your set. Remember to decide on the direction of play. Choose teams and give each player a mallet and a ball of the same color.

HITTING THE BALL

To hit your ball, stand just behind it and bend your knees. Draw the mallet back between your legs and then let it swing forward. Hit the ball low, in the center. Striking the ball from the side as in golf is legal but less accurate.

Whack an opponent's ball by placing your ball beside hers, putting your foot on your own ball and smashing your ball with the mallet to send the other ball flying.

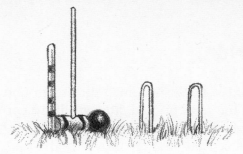

1.
The player with the black mallet goes first. She places her ball one mallet-head from the starting stake. She hits the ball to send it through the first hoop. If successful, she gets another turn to try for the second hoop. She keeps on until her ball doesn't go through a hoop.

2.
White, usually the second player and from the opposing team, starts as Black did. If he clears the first hoop, he can try for the second *or* try to hit black's ball with his.

3.

If White misses Black's ball, his turn is over. If he hits Black's ball, he gets two more turns, one to whack Black's ball and one to try for the next hoop.

4.

White can then go through his next hoop or try to hit a different player's ball. But he must go through his next hoop before going after Black's ball again. White continues until he misses a hoop or ball.

5.

The rest of the players take their turns, choosing to drive through hoops or hit an opponent's ball. Players' balls have to tap the stake at the halfway point and at home too for their turn to continue.

6.

Once someone has finished the course and has only the home stake to hit, he can rove the course hitting and whacking opponents' balls, over and over, for extra turns without having to go through hoops. A rover's turn ends with a missed hit.

7.

A team wins when every member goes through all hoops and hits the home stake before the whole opposing team does.

TIPS

- Don't smash the ball — a steady stroke and good aim make the best shot.

- If a ball is hit through a hoop by anyone but its owner, it doesn't count. So try hitting your opponent's ball with your own through all the hoops to home. You accumulate extra turns and move your opponent's ball far from its next hoop.

BOCCE BALL

Bocce is a game of outdoor bowling that can be played on whatever ground is available — a few bushes and rocks just add to the challenge. To play, you'll need a set of eight bocce balls, a jack, or target ball, and two teams of up to four players each.

PLAYING THE GAME

Each player gets one or two balls, depending on the number playing. Decide on the throwing line, boundaries and who goes first. When one player is bowling, the others must stand behind the throwing line.

1.

The lead player tosses the jack from the throwing line to the far end of the green. Then the same player bowls one ball, trying to make it stop as near the jack as possible and stay in bounds. It doesn't matter if the jack is hit as long as it remains in bounds.

2.

The second team now bowls. Players on that team take turns until one of their balls lands closer to the jack than the starting team's ball. A bowl can be a toss, a roll or an aerial "bomb" — whichever will get the ball closest to the jack.

3.

If the jack is hit out of bounds, return it to where it lay before the last shot was taken. If a ball is bowled or hit out of bounds, it stays out.

4.

Once the second team gets a ball closer than the first, the starting team tries to get a ball closer still.

5.

The round ends when all balls have been bowled. Sometimes, one team runs out of balls early and the other team gets to bowl the last few balls in a row. The score is tallied and the balls are collected.

6.

The team that didn't toss the jack in the first round gets to lead in the second one.

SCORING

When all the balls have been played, a point is scored for every ball sitting closer to the jack than the opponents' closest ball. The game is over at 12, 16 or 21 points — decide before you start to play.

TIPS

- There is usually a colored spot on a bocce ball. The ball will curve in the direction of the spot if it is rolled with the spot on the side. The ball will travel a straighter course if the spot is on top.

- Try cornering the jack in rocks and shrubs and then placing your balls to block out the opposition.

- If your opponents block you, try bombing their ball — or bomb the jack so it moves closer to your balls.

A TWO-THOUSAND-YEAR-OLD GAME

Roman soldiers played bocce and took it with them wherever their armies traveled. Now bocce, or the French version, *jeu de boules*, is played worldwide.

BADMINTON

Badminton is a great game because, with practice, anyone can make powerful shots. This unofficial version can be played by two or four people on any flat, grassy area about 6 m x 14 m (20 ft. x 45 ft.) that is protected from the wind. You'll need a badminton racket for each player, a birdie and a tightly strung net (about 2.5 m, or 8 ft. high) that cuts the court in half.

PLAYING THE GAME

Players should agree on boundary lines for the whole court and inside lines for the service courts. Use tufts of grass, pebbles or tree roots as markers.

1.

In singles, each player starts the game standing on the right side of his court. The first server hits the birdie diagonally over the net to land inside the opponent's right service court. The serve is an underhand stroke, with the birdie hit below the server's waist.

2.

If the serve is fair, the opponent tries to return it over the net to land anywhere on the server's side of the net — not just in the little service court.

3.

The birdie is played back and forth until one side loses by missing a shot, hitting the birdie into the net or out of bounds, or by hitting the birdie more than once before sending it over the net.

4.

If the server loses, it's the opponent's turn to serve. If the server wins, she gets a point and serves again, this time from the left service court. The game proceeds with the server switching service courts after each point won.

5.

A doubles game follows the same rules as singles. Partners stand side by side and each tries to play shots coming into his side of the court. When one team serves and wins a point, the server moves from the right to the left service court, switching places with her partner. When a team loses the serve and then wins it back, the partner who didn't serve last time gets to serve from the side he is in.

SCORING

Only the side serving in badminton can score, one point per winning shot. When the serving side loses the serve, it is the other side's turn to serve and try to earn points. Games are usually to 15 points.

BALLOONMINTON

A fun variation of badminton uses balloons instead of birdies. Blow balloons partway up and dribble in some water before tying the end. Use old, inexpensive rackets in this game in case the balloon bursts and wets the strings.

BOOTIN'

If you're a hockey fanatic who lives and breathes the game all year long, bootin' is the game for you. The equipment is simple: hockey sticks, a soft ball the size of a melon and boots, of course. Boots act as shin pads and feet protectors.

PLAYING THE GAME

Set out the boundaries of the play area, whether it is a lawn, beach, park or school-yard. A rectangular space is ideal but not necessary. Trees, rocks, buildings and hazards should be declared out of bounds.

Set up a goal the size of a regular hockey net at either end of the play area.

1.
Divide into two teams of three to eight players each. Use different kinds of clothing to tell the teams apart — one team plays in T-shirts, the other in swimsuits.

2.
Teams choose a goalie and one or two players to play defense. The rest are forwards.

3.
The ball is placed on the ground in the center of the play area. Two players, one from each team, "face off" saying together, "one, two, three, go" and try to gain possession of the ball.

4.
Players try to get the ball past the goalie of the opposite team. Each goal counts for one point.

RULES

- Highsticking is not allowed. The blade of the stick must stay below the knees and the handle of the stick below the shoulder.

- If a player is hit with a stick anywhere except on the boots, he can take a free shot on the goalie, ten paces out from the net. All the other players stand aside.

- For safety, players are not allowed to raise the ball off the ground higher than their knees.

HOCKEY HYDRATION

Even on ice, hockey players get hot and thirsty. Don't forget to drink plenty of water when playing bootin' or any other outdoor game in the summer. At the end of the game, douse off with a hose or ask an adult if you can go swimming. You can choose the three stars of the game once you're all wet.

5.
When one team hits the ball out of bounds, a member of the other team places the ball on the boundary line where it went out and shoots it back into play.

6.
In bootin' there are no periods or intermissions. The game continues until everyone is exhausted. Each game ends in a tie, no matter how many goals have been scored. When ready to stop, one player calls, "last goal ties."

GOOFY GOLF

The makings of a miniature-golf course are hiding in your home. Scavenge through the shed, kitchen cupboards and toy box and you'll find prefabricated obstacles. Then the only other things you'll need are a golf ball and a putter for each player. If you don't have putters, use hockey sticks, croquet mallets or umbrellas instead.

GETTING READY

- Ask an adult to help you set up your golf course. Make flags from straightened coat hangers and triangles of paper.

- Choose an outdoor play area to set up your course — a lawn, park or playing field will do. You don't need a large area. Fairways can zigzag back and forth across one another. It's easier to putt on grass that is short. Make use of what your play area has to offer — shots can go under a tree, over a mound of earth, along a smooth path and so on.

- Establish a starting line and lay out a continuous course of nine "holes" with one obstacle and one flag per hole. Use the flag plus stones or wooden sticks as pegs to hold any wobbly obstacles in place.

AN EAVES-TROUGH-PIPE ELBOW

BUILDING-BLOCK GATES

A NATURAL HOLE

A TIN CAN OPEN AT BOTH ENDS

1 M (3 FT.) OF DRYER HOSE

START

A WOODEN RAMP

8

6

9

FINISH

A TIN CAN AND PINWHEEL

FOUR CROQUET HOOPS

4

3

TWO PIECES OF THICK WOOD

PLAYING THE GAME

Choose one player to go first. She shoots her golf ball from the starting line to the first hole and through it, keeping track of the number of shots she takes. All other players do the same. Don't pick up your golf ball between holes, just putt to the next obstacle. Continue until each player has completed the course. The player with the lowest score is the winner.

Store the parts of the game in a box or return borrowed obstacles at the end of the game.

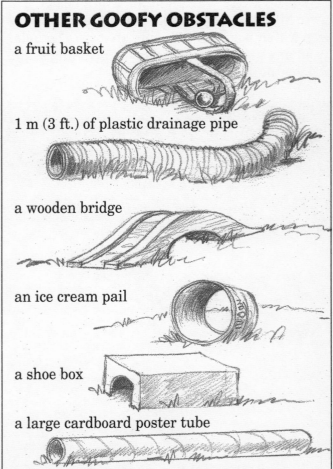

OTHER GOOFY OBSTACLES

a fruit basket

1 m (3 ft.) of plastic drainage pipe

a wooden bridge

an ice cream pail

a shoe box

a large cardboard poster tube

25

FRISBEE GOLF

Are you ready for the challenge of Frisbee golf? This crazy summer game borrows from traditional golf, but no golfing experience is required.

GETTING READY

Plan the course with the help of an adult. Try to include a variety of terrains such as a beach, a lawn, hills and rocks. Make sure hazards such as deep water, poison ivy or cliffs are out of bounds. Avoid any neighbors' property — including their prize petunias.

You'll need:
nine Frisbee-sized circles of cardboard
felt markers
tape and thumbtacks
a Frisbee for each player or team
a pencil
paper for scorecards

1.
Label the cardboard circles, or "flags," with the numbers 1 through 9.

2.
Choose a starting line and place the first flag about 25 steps away. Tape or tack the flag about 1 m (3 ft.) above the ground on a tree, a rock or the side of a building. Choose a spot to post the second flag, about 25 steps from the first. Continue until you have placed all nine circles. It's okay if the paths cross one another.

3.

Walk the course to decide on the number of shots each "hole" should take. This is called the par. Easy holes are par 2, more difficult ones, par 3. If a hole is on very difficult terrain and will take several lucky shots to get there, call it a par 4. Mark the par on each flag.

PLAYING THE GAME

- Each player throws the Frisbee from the starting line, trying to strike the first flag. If he misses, he takes his next shot from the place where his Frisbee landed. Count up the number of tosses it takes and record it on your scorecard. Take turns so all players complete each hole before you go on to the next.

- The object of the game is to finish the course with the lowest score. It may take several rounds before you get a good score.

- If it is too difficult to score par on a hole, increase the par. If it is too easy, reduce the par.

MORE

HOW TO THROW A FRISBEE

Grasp the Frisbee by the outside rim, placing your thumb along the edge as shown. Cross your arm over your chest and bend your knees a little. Swing the Frisbee forward, releasing it at hip level as you straighten your legs. Practice until you have perfected the standard Frisbee throw. Soon, you'll be able to control how far you throw the Frisbee and the direction of your throw.

RULES

- If you throw your Frisbee into water, add one penalty shot to your score. Retrieve your Frisbee with an adult watching.

- You're allowed one "Mulligan" per round of nine holes. That means if you make a terrible shot, you can take it again without counting it.

- Don't walk in front of other players while they are taking their turns. If you interfere with a shot, you add one point to your score and the player takes the shot over.

- If the family dog runs off with your Frisbee, mark your spot and chase him. No penalty!

PAR FOR THE PARK

If it's not possible to lay out an organized course, create the game as you play. Take turns deciding which object to aim for next and how many throws are allowed. Keep score in your head.

Hit the fountain in four

HIDING GAMES

Hiding outdoors provides the perfect opportunity for daydreaming or watching the natural world around you. But keep your wits about you so you'll be ready for the dash to home base.

HIDE-AND-SEEK

1.
Choose a home base — a tree or a back step is perfect.

2.
One person is It. The other players hide. If you're hiding, choose a spot where you will be safe and well camouflaged. It's best if you can see home base.

3.
It covers his eyes and counts loudly and slowly. When he reaches 25, he shouts, "Ready or not, here I come," and the search is on.

4.
When It sees someone, he shouts that player's name: "One, two, three on Madeline!" and they both race back to home base. If It wins the race, the caught player must help find the others. If the caught player reaches home base first, she is "home free" and doesn't help look for the others.

5.
The game is over when every person has been found. The one who was caught first is It for the next game.

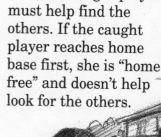

MORE

KICK THE CAN

This version of the game is played like regular hide-and-seek, but home base is a tin can. Caught players stand beside the can until a hiding player sneaks back to home base, kicks the can, and frees all caught players. If a player is tagged by It while trying to kick the can, or if It gets to the can first, she is caught too. The game continues until all hiding players are found and standing beside the can. This can take a long time!

NOCTURNAL HIDE-AND-SEEK

For nocturnal hide-and-seek you'll need a flashlight and three or more players dressed in dark clothing. Before you play, decide on a home base and boundaries with the help of an adult. Make all hazardous areas — such as roadways, water and patches of poison ivy — out of bounds.

1.
Choose a person to be It. Standing at home base with the flashlight, It covers her eyes and counts to 25, slowly and loudly. The other players sneak off into the night to hide. When It reaches 25, she shouts, "Ready or not, here I come," and looks for the hiding players.

Ready or not, here I come!

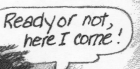

2.
When It sees a player, she shines the light on him and calls out his name. He is caught and goes to home base. Other hiding players can try to free people from home base by touching them, being careful not to get caught in the flashlight beam themselves.

3.
The game continues until all players are caught and back at home base. In this game, the last person to be "beamed" is It.

All-e-all-e-in-free!

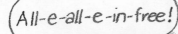

4.
If the last player is hidden too well and can't be found, call out, "all-e-all-e-in-free" to let him know the game is over and he won't become It.

HIDE AND SQUISH

One person hides in a snug spot, such as a garden shed, behind a woodpile, or under a low-branched tree while the others count out loud to 25. The players split up to look for the hidden player. As each person finds the hiding spot, she quietly climbs in. When all the players are squished in, the game is over. The first person to find the hiding spot starts the next squish.

WINTER HIDEOUTS

In northern climates, many species of snakes have "squishes" of their own. They hibernate in groups, choosing protected places such as rock gardens, rotting stumps and old wells. Canada is home to the world's largest snake squish. More than 10 000 red-sided garter snakes snuggle closely together in Manitoba's underground caverns from September until April.

SCAVENGER HUNT

Every scavenger hunt is a one-of-a-kind event — the fun lies in the hunting and in making up a crazy adaptation to suit your summer space. If you and a group of friends create one, together you supervise the hunt and decide on the winner. You'll need a pencil and paper, at least six friends divided into two or more teams, a bag for each team to collect things in, and a large, interesting outdoor space.

GETTING READY

- Ask an adult what places are unsafe and declare them out of bounds. Depending on where you are, unsafe areas could be across the street or near the lake. Homes are usually out of bounds too.

- For an hour-long hunt, make a list of about 30 things to collect. Include some items that should be easy to find. Add some that are harder to locate or will take a little thinking. Then, include some impossible things that kids may have to invent. You can star hard-to-find items and offer a bonus point for each of them.

1 wet towel
5 smooth stones
2 horse feathers
exactly 57 of something *
4 round leaves
1 solar collector
1 dirty sock
2 bikini bottoms
1 piece of kindling
6 bear paws *
1 yummy dessert
1 dandelion flower
a fastener *

PLAYING THE GAME

At the beginning of the game, set a time limit and give each team a list of items to find and a bag. Make sure everyone knows the rules:

- all items must be found or borrowed with permission, nothing should be stolen or bought just for the game

- players must stay outdoors and in bounds

When time is up, each team presents its findings, as convincingly as possible, to the other participants. Total the points and bonus points to decide which team wins.

ABC SCAVENGER HUNT

In this quick and easy hunt, everyone can play, even the organizers. Players decide on a time limit, for example, 30 minutes. Then each player or team takes a bag and heads off to find one item that begins with each letter of the alphabet. The person or team that finds the most items in the time set, wins.

WILD SCAVENGERS

Vultures are scavengers that feed on dead and rotting animals. They soar high in the air and find their deliciously putrid meals by smelling them out. Unless you have an unusually keen sense of smell, you'll find most items in a scavenger hunt using your eyes — you'll rarely sniff one out.

TREASURE HUNT

A treasure hunt is a good event to organize if you're having friends of different ages over. All you need is a shovel, a pencil and paper, and treasure. The treasure should include energy food and drinks because everyone will be hungry by the time it's unearthed!

The best treasure hunts get friends working together, not against one another. If you can, wrap the loot well and bury it in the ground. The organizer of a hunt can't play but can dig into the spoils at the end.

GETTING READY

1.

Choose a big playing area and decide where to start the hunt and where to bury the loot. A good burying place is a dug-up garden, in a spot where there are no plants growing.

2.

Survey the whole playing area and choose ten places to hide clues. In each place you will leave a clue that should lead the treasure hunters to the next clue.

3.

Write ten clues. Your clues should be hard but solvable by your hunters. If you want players to look under the seat of the swing, for instance, you could write a word scramble for "swing seat," you could draw a map or you could write a riddle such as "where one seat meets another" — it all depends on the age of your treasure hunters.

4.

When no one is watching, lay out all your clues in order, except the first one. Then walk through the sequence to make sure every clue is in the right place. Bury the treasure and invite your friends over.

5.

Give them the first clue and a shovel. Be sure you're around at the end to share the treasure!

SKULL AND CROSSBONES

No treasure hunt is complete without a pirate theme. While you're planning the hunt, others can be making a traditional skull-and-crossbones flag, eye patches or bandannas so they can really act the part.

35

CAPTURE THE FLAG

There are flags on top of mountains and on the Moon. They flutter back and forth proclaiming, "We did it, we were here!" Capture the flag is a game of speed, strategy and patience. Be prepared to stand guard for your flag or risk prison to snatch your opponents'. Set up generous but safe boundaries, choose two teams of at least three people, find or make a flag for each team, and you're ready for action.

PLAYING THE GAME

Capture the flag can be played on a playing field or a beach, or in a park or a large garden. Use a garden hose or rope to divide the play area in half. Mark a line 1 m (3 ft.) on each side. The space between these two lines is the safe zone.

1.

Each team chooses a tree branch or pole on which to fly its flag. The flag must be visible.

2.

The object of the game is to find and capture the flag of the opposing team and return it to your territory, without being touched. At the same time, each team tries to protect its own flag.

3.

If a player crosses into the opponents' territory and is touched by a player on that team, he becomes a prisoner and must sit near the opponents' flag. A teammate can free prisoners by sneaking in and touching them. The rescuer and rescued players must return to their own side before attempting to capture the flag.

4.

Work as a team with a plan of attack. Leave at least one player guarding your own flag. Distract your opponents with loud noises or by running in a zigzag manner. When they're off guard, race in and snatch their flag. Be ready to sprint back to the safe zone if you're spotted.

5.

The team whose players capture the opponents' flag and safely return with it to their own territory, wins.

TIPS

- In defending the flag or in trying to capture your opponents' flag, be sneaky. It is best not to be seen.

- It is hard to defend your flag and win this game if your teammates are captured. Rescue them first, snatch the flag later.

- If you are playing with a large group, members of one team should wear something to identify them, such as a bandanna or hat.

FLAG SIGNALS

For more than 5000 years people have used flags to send messages. Flags can signal retreat, surrender or charge, friend or foe, good news or bad, keep out, or quarantine.

If capture the flag has gone on for hours and you are ready for lunch, wave a white flag. It's the international signal for a truce.

TAG

"**Y**ou're It!" And the chase is on. Tag is played by people worldwide and by many animals too. It's good exercise and requires little or no equipment. You probably already know how to play the basic game, so here are some wild summertime variations to choose from.

RATTLESNAKE TAG

A rattlesnake tail rattles but doesn't bite, so it's safe to attach yourself to this end.

1.
Choose someone to be It. The other players line up behind one person, the "head," holding onto the waist of the player in front to form a snake. The last person in the line is the rattle.

2.
It tries to catch and hold onto the rattle's waist. If she is successful, the head of the snake becomes It.

3.
If anyone in the line lets go, he is automatically It. If there are more than five players, form two snakes but have only one It. Both snakes try to slither out of reach.

PUDDING TAG

FLAG TAG

"I got you!" "No you didn't." Sounds familiar, right? Here's a game of tag that's cheat-proof. The proof is in the pudding.

You'll need:

a small plastic bowl of pudding

three or more players dressed in swimsuits

a hose

1.
Place the bowl of pudding at home base — a picnic table is perfect.

2.
Choose someone to be It. It counts to 10 while the other players scatter, then dips his finger in the pudding and gives chase. You know you're It when there's a smear of pudding on you.

3.
When the game is over, hose off all the pudding.

If you don't have any pudding, try flag tag. Choose an It. All players, except It, tuck a bandanna into their waistband or back pocket. It gives a getaway count of 25. When It catches up with a player, she grabs his bandanna, puts it in her back pocket, and runs away. The new It chases after someone else's bandanna. The bandannas can change hands quickly, so watch out. You never know who might be It.

39

JUST FOR ONE OR TWO

When the active outdoor games are over, relax in the shade. Some of the best summer games can be played there, by yourself or with one friend. This section is full of games for one or two.

When you're alone, practice your gaming skills. Learn to shuffle cards or roll marbles like a pro. Work on stunts such as juggling or card tricks.

Games for two can be fast and full of laughter. Think of a crazy saying for hangman, whack your king down fast in double solitaire or whip your friend at checkers — again!

JUGGLING

How many objects can you keep in the air at once? One? Two? Juggling isn't as easy as it looks. It takes special training and concentration. Keep your eye on the ball and practice, practice, practice.

Try juggling small beanbags or nonbouncy balls, such as old tennis balls. Whichever you choose, you must be able to hold two in one hand. Start with one ball and work your way up to two or three.

JUGGLE ONE

1.

Hold one ball in your "comfy" hand, or dominant hand. Throw the ball up in an arch and catch it with your other hand. Pass the ball back to your comfy hand and repeat, over and over again.

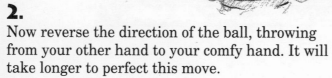

2.

Now reverse the direction of the ball, throwing from your other hand to your comfy hand. It will take longer to perfect this move.

JUGGLE TWO

1.
When you feel ready, move on to two balls. Hold one ball in the fingertips of each hand. Toss the ball from your comfy hand up in an arch toward your other hand. When this ball reaches the top of the arch, toss the ball from your other hand toward your comfy hand, below the arch of the first ball. Catch the balls. Practice this move.

2.
Talk to yourself and get a rhythm going in your head. Saying "one, two, one, two, one, two" will help.

3.
Now practice the reverse motion, throwing from your other hand first. Keep doing this continuous motion until you've perfected it. You'll be chasing balls until you get the hang of it.

JUGGLE THREE

1.
To add a third ball, place two in the comfy hand and one in the other. Toss one ball from your comfy hand in a high arch toward the other hand. When the ball is at the top of the arch, throw the ball from the other hand back toward the comfy hand. When that ball is at the top and starting to come down, toss the third ball. Catch all the balls. Now you should have two balls in your other hand and one in your comfy hand. Return one to your comfy hand and repeat.

2.
Continue practicing. Once you have perfected this move, try to keep the three balls in the air in continuous motion. Say "one, two, three" over and over to yourself.

Now you know what someone means when she says "I have three balls in the air" — she's busy!

43

SKILLFUL STUNTS

What can you do with a coin, a spoon and a lazy afternoon? Practice these simple stunts and dazzle your family with a display of your craft by dinnertime. This may be the beginning of a promising career or just a fun way to pass the summer hours.

MATHEMAGICAL SPOONS

Two spoons and a pair of hands is all it takes to make math magic.

1.
Sit on the ground or at a table and ask your family or friends to gather 'round. Explain that you will be demonstrating a number with your magic spoons. Their job is to guess the number and say it aloud, but not say how they got the number.

2.
Lay the spoons on the ground in a random pattern. Tell your audience that the spoons are showing a number between one and ten.

3.
Rest your hands on either side of the spoons, with some fingers folded under and some lying flat. The number of visible fingers indicates the magic number.

4.
If no one guesses, reveal the number and repeat the trick, showing a different number. Eventually, someone will catch on and become your assistant. Keep going until everyone has figured out the trick. Don't be surprised if a younger sibling or friend wants to demonstrate the trick next. Play along, even though you've got his number.

DISAPPEARING COINS

Where did that quarter go? How did it vanish into your arm and reappear somewhere else? Keep your friends guessing with this trick — your success will depend on how quickly you can maneuver. Remember, the hand is quicker than the eye.

1.
Sit with your left elbow on a table and your left hand resting nonchalantly on your shoulder.

2.
With a dramatic flourish, pick up a coin with your right hand. Explain to your audience that you will make the coin disappear into your left forearm and reappear somewhere else on your body.

3.
Rub the coin on your left arm. Appear to be serious and concentrating.

4.
Drop the coin and quickly put both hands on the table. Pretend to retrieve the coin with your right hand as you secretly pick it up with your left hand. Place the coin on your shoulder while continuing to rub your forearm with your right hand.

5.
After several seconds, open your right hand and exclaim that the coin has vanished. Pick it off your left shoulder and show the amazed crowd.

GET READY TO DEAL

Cards were played by Chinese royalty more than a thousand years ago. These rulers even put their faces on the cards. You don't have to be royal to play, but by learning these skills, you'll be on your way to becoming a master at cards. That's enough to royally scare any opponent.

THE DECK

There are 52 cards in a deck, divided into four suits: two red (hearts and diamonds) and two black (spades and clubs). In some games, such as bridge, the suits have different values. Spades are high followed by hearts, diamonds and finally clubs. Each suit has 13 cards with an ace, 2, 3, 4, 5, 6, 7, 8, 9, 10, jack, queen and king. In many games these last three cards, the face cards, are worth the most. Ace is usually the highest, but in some games ace is the lowest.

Decks often come with two jokers. They can be used in place of lost cards or as wild cards. A wild card is any card that has been assigned a special value or function in the game. In some games a player who has a wild card can use it in place of any other card in the deck.

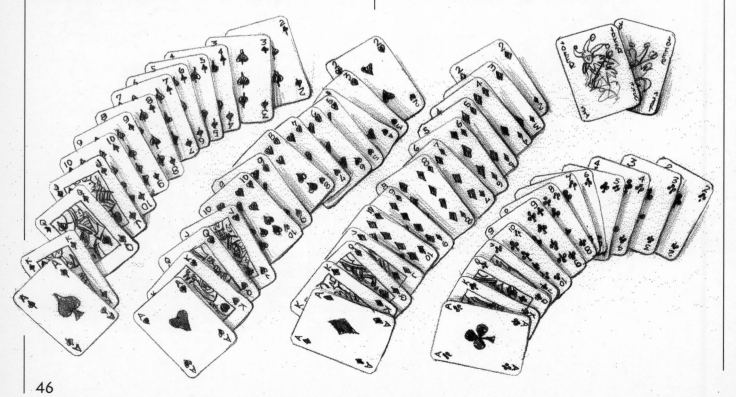

THE DEALER

In most card games, one person will deal, or pass around, the cards. To choose the first dealer, lay the deck facedown on the table. Each player picks a card from anywhere in the deck. The highest card wins the deal. The second dealer is the person to the left of the first dealer.

SHUFFLING

Before each new hand, the dealer usually shuffles, or mixes up, the deck while holding the cards facedown. There are no rules about shuffling, but there are two basic methods.

SIMPLE SHUFFLE

Hold the deck, by the ends, in your right hand, supported below by the left hand. Lift up the right hand, leaving a small wedge of cards resting on the left hand. Bring the right hand forward and drop the deck, or a few cards at a time, in front of the cards held in the left hand. Repeat this twenty times to shuffle the deck thoroughly. (Left-handed people may need to reverse the hands.)

MORE

SHUFFLE CASCADE

1.

Divide the deck into two even piles, one for each hand. Hold each pile with your thumb on one end, index finger bent on the middle of the back of the card pile and the remaining three fingers along the other end of the pile, resting on the table.

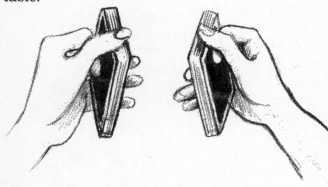

2.

While pushing down with the index-finger knuckles, lift your thumbs and bring them together so they are touching. Let go of the cards, a few at a time, at the thumb ends only until they are all woven together.

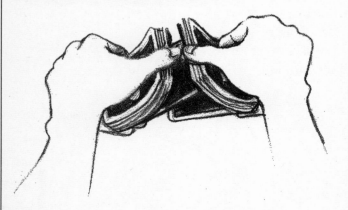

3.

Lay the cards flat on the table and slide the deck together again. Repeat ten times to shuffle the deck thoroughly.

4.

When you have perfected this skill, you can impress your friends by replacing step 3 with a flourish. Place both thumbs side by side on top of the middle of the pile. Keep the thumbs firmly in place and slide your fingers under the cards. Use the ridges where your fingers meet your palms to push the outer edges of the cards toward each other. Bend the cards up in an arch. Straighten your index fingers to get them out of the way of the cards and relax your fingers. Then gently push down with both thumbs. With practice, the cards will cascade into a neat pile.

CUTTING THE DECK

The dealer places the deck on the table in front of the person to his right. She can choose to cut or not cut the cards. To cut, she lifts part of the deck off the top and places it to the right on the table, making two piles. Then she lifts the left-hand pile and covers the right-hand pile. If she decides not to cut, she taps the top of the deck with her knuckles. This indicates she is happy to leave the cards as they are.

DEALING

The dealer's job is to pass out the required number of cards. Holding the deck facedown, he deals one card to the person on his left, one card to the next player and then the next, continuing in a circle. If the face of any card is exposed, a misdeal can be declared. The cards are then reshuffled, cut and dealt again.

DRAW PILE

In most games, the cards left over after the deal are placed neatly, facedown as a draw pile. When a player is required to take another card, she takes the top card off this pile.

DISCARD PILE

This is the companion to the draw pile. Cards that are discarded from a player's hand or drawn but not wanted are placed faceup in a neat stack beside the draw pile. When all the cards from the draw pile are in the discard pile, it is turned over to become the draw pile again. The rules of each game specify if these cards are shuffled or left in their existing order.

49

CARD TRICKS

When you have some time to yourself and a deck of cards, it's the perfect opportunity to learn some card tricks. Practice each trick over and over until you have it mastered. Then polish your performance by adding interesting spoken lines and even a costume. It's best never to repeat a trick, so learn a second one for an encore.

♠ ♥ ♦ ♣ ♠ ♥ ♦ ♣ ♠ ♥ ♦ ♣ ♠ ♥

MAGIC KEY CARD

The more you can involve the members of your audience in this trick, the more amazed they will be. But you must keep your eye on where the key card is at all times.

1.

Ask one spectator to shuffle a deck of cards (see pages 47 and 48). When you take the deck back, hold it on its side for a moment so you can see the bottom card without being obvious. Memorize the card: it is your "key" card.

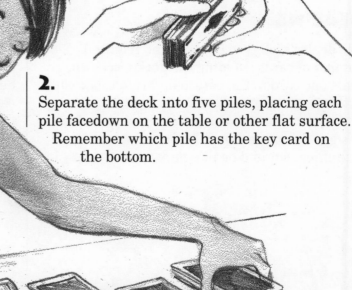

2.

Separate the deck into five piles, placing each pile facedown on the table or other flat surface. Remember which pile has the key card on the bottom.

3.

Ask a spectator to lift the top card off any pile, look at it and even show others, without showing you. Then ask her to memorize the card and put it back down on its pile.

4.

Now, pick up the pile with the key card in it and place it on top of the pile your friend chose. That puts the key card on top of the card your friend chose. Then add all the other piles in any order.

5.

If, in step 3, the spectator happens to pick the top card of the pile that has the key card in it, ask her to slip it, facedown, under that pile. You know the key card is now on top of your friend's chosen card. Put the pile with the key card in it on top of any other pile and add all the other piles, in any order.

6.

Ask another spectator to cut the deck (see page 49) twice. Chances are two cuts will not separate the key card from your friend's card.

7.

Now, holding the deck facedown, slowly deal out the cards faceup, watching for the key card. The next card after it will be the card you're looking for. This is a good part of the trick to jazz up by pretending the cards are talking to you, by going past the chosen card and returning to it, or by adding your own flourishes.

MORE

◆ ♥ ◆ ♣ ♠ ♥ ◆ ♣ ♠ ♥ ◆ ♣ ♠ ♥ ◆ ♣ ♠ ♥ ◆ ♣ ♠ ♥ ◆ ♣ ♠ ♥ ◆ ♣

SUMMER PARTY CARD TRICK

This trick works because people confuse cutting a deck of cards with shuffling a deck of cards. It is best if you tell a little story along with it — one is suggested in the directions, but you can make up your own. The trick uses only the aces, kings, queens and jacks from a deck of cards.

1.

Arrange the cards so all the aces are together, then all the kings, queens and jacks, in that order. Turn the deck facedown. Say, "One family, the Aces, invited friends over for a barbecue at their summer place by the lake."

2.

Start dealing the aces out into four piles in a row. As you put each card down, pretend each one is a family member and say, "The mother started the fire for the barbecue, the father cut veggies in the kitchen, the son set the picnic table outside and the daughter went to her room to practice card tricks."

3.

Then put a king on top of each of the aces and say, "Their friends the Kingstons were the first to arrive. One went to help with the barbecue, one to the kitchen, one outside to the picnic table and one to find the daughter in her room."

4.

In the same way, deal out the queens and jacks — the Queens family and the Jackson family — and explain where they go. Then say, "See, here all the families have divided up and not one family member is with another. Someone says, 'Let's have lunch.'"

5.
Pick up all four piles, putting them on top of each other. Turn the pile facedown on the table and start cutting the cards (p. 49). Do complete cuts, so the bottom of the cut is always put over the top. *Do not* shuffle the cards. Say, "The families mingle with each other, eating, cleaning up, going for a swim, watching a magic show…"

6.
Deal the cards, still facedown, into four piles again, making sure you deal in the same direction the whole time. Say, "Finally, everyone is tired and gets ready to go home."

7.
Turn over each pile to show the aces all together in one pile, and the same with the kings, queens and jacks. With a little surprise in your voice, say, "And see, even though they were separated as families and then mixed in the big group all afternoon, when it's time to leave, the family members find each other without any trouble."

53

RUMMY

When you're old enough to sort and hold ten cards, you're ready to take on anyone in this version of rummy. It's possible to play with three or four players, but it's more fun to go head to head with one opponent.

THE OBJECT OF THE GAME

The first person to lay down his cards, with all ten arranged in a combination of runs of the same suit and groups of the same number, wins.

Runs: three or more cards that follow in sequence

Groups: three or four cards of the same number

PLAYING THE GAME

1.

Decide who will be the first dealer. She shuffles, her opponent cuts, and she deals out ten cards each, then deals her opponent one more, for a total of eleven. The rest of the deck is placed facedown on the table. (When playing with more people, deal seven cards each and turn over the top card to start a draw pile. The person to the dealer's left goes first.)

2.

Organize your hand into suits, then see if there are runs and groups within the hand. In rummy, aces are low.

3.

The player with eleven cards discards one, faceup, to form the discard pile beside the draw pile.

4.

The dealer picks up either the top card from the discard pile or the top one from the draw pile. If the card helps to make a run or group, she keeps it and discards one she doesn't need. If the draw card is not needed, she discards it. Once she discards, her turn is over.

Your turn.

5.

If you get to the bottom of the draw pile, turn the discard pile over, unshuffled, and play through the deck again.

6.

Continue taking turns until all the cards in one player's hand are in runs and groups. He ends the game by discarding one card facedown, laying his hand faceup on the table and calling, "Rummy!"

SHOUT IT OUT

"Rummy" is the traditional thing to say when you win this game. Some people shout "gin," while others may say "Dixie bell." Dream up your own fun expression that will let everyone know you have won.

Gin!

SCORING

Each face card is worth 10 points.

Ace through 10 are worth their face value:
      ace = 1 point
      2 = 2 points
      10 = 10 points

Rummy = 50 points

This winning hand is worth 114 points.

MARATHON CARD GAMES

Snap and war are two card games that can last for hours. You'll need quick reflexes and plenty of time to win.

SNAP

Have you got a drawer full of old cards — two or more decks with a few cards missing from each? Mix them together to make the perfect snap deck. Now all you need is one friend and a place where you can make lots of noise.

PLAYING THE GAME

1.
Players sit opposite each other. One person deals out all the cards, facedown, into two draw piles, one in front of each player.

2.
Ready, set, go. Players turn over one card each at the same time and place it faceup in a pile beside their draw pile.

3.
This is repeated until the two cards are of the same value. The first person to yell, "Snap!" wins all the faceup cards. These are placed facedown at the bottom of her draw pile.

4.
Play resumes as before. When all the cards in a player's draw pile have been turned faceup, the player leaves the top card faceup on the table and turns the rest of the cards over, making a new draw pile. The game continues until one person has all the cards.

ANIMAL SNAP

Crank up the noise level of this already raucous game by assigning each player an animal such as a pig, dog or cow. Instead of saying "snap," players must make the appropriate noise — grunt, bark, moo and so on. The first player to make her noise gets all the faceup cards. If a player gets mixed up and makes the wrong animal noise or says "snap," he loses all the cards in his faceup pile.

♠♥ ♦♣♠♠♥ ♦♣♠♠♥ ♦♣♠♥ ♦♣♠♥ ♦♣♠♥ ♦♣♠♥

WAR

There's no shooting or prisoners in this game of war — only two friends trying to win all the cards.

PLAYING THE GAME

1.
Players sit opposite each other. One person deals out a complete deck of 52 cards into two piles facedown on the table.

2.
Cards are valued in order, with 2 carrying the lowest value and ace the highest. All suits are equal.

3.
At the same time, each player turns over the top card on his pile. The person with the highest card wins both cards and sets them aside, facedown in a winnings pile.

4.
Players continue as above until the two upturned cards are of the same value. War is now declared. Each player draws the next three cards from the top of his pile and places them facedown on the table. The fourth card is drawn and turned faceup. The highest card wins both piles of four. If the cards are the same again, the process is repeated until one card is higher. The winner takes all the cards used in this war.

5.
When all the cards in the draw piles have been won or lost, players shuffle their winnings piles and keep playing. The game continues until one person has won all the cards.

WAR

DOUBLE SOLITAIRE

The perfect recipe for solitary entertainment: one person, one deck of cards and a rainy afternoon. Have twice the fun by adding another person and a second, different deck of cards for a game of double solitaire.

THE DEAL

One player says "go" and each player deals out from the top of her deck as follows:

- Turn one card faceup on a flat surface, followed by six cards facedown to start seven piles.

- Continue with one up on the second pile and one down on each of the other five piles; one up, four down; one up, three down; one up, two down; one up, one down; ending with one up.

- The remaining cards are placed facedown in a draw pile to one side. Straighten all the piles, leaving a space in the middle, between the two players' piles.

PLAYING THE GAME

1.

As soon as each player completes the deal, she begins to play, moving as many dealt cards as she can, arranging them in descending order, alternating red and black. For example, a red jack can be placed on top of a black queen. Players cannot move a card to place it *under* another card.

2.

When a player exposes a facedown card, she can turn it over and move it to another pile if possible.

3.

Any ace that comes up is placed in the middle to begin a foundation pile. The 2 of that suit can be placed on top, followed by the other cards in order as they come up. Each player tries to get all of her cards onto the foundation cards. Players can build on any of the eight foundation piles.

4.

When one of the seven dealt piles is empty, the player can move a king and any other cards on top of it over to fill the space and expose the facedown card they covered.

5.

When no more dealt cards can be moved, each player turns over her draw-pile cards, three at a time, placing them faceup in a discard pile. Only the top card on the discard pile can be played on the foundation cards or one of the seven dealt piles.

6.

When all the cards in the draw pile have been exposed, turn them over and run through the pile again. Never shuffle the draw pile.

7.

The game is over when one player plays all her cards from the dealt piles onto the foundation cards and is declared the winner, or when neither player can make a move. If this happens, the foundation cards are sorted into two decks and counted. The person who played the most cards onto the foundation piles wins.

CHECKERS

You've just been crowned queen — or is that king? You turn around quickly, spot an enemy and lunge — just as your mother approaches with glasses of cold lemonade. To enjoy a real-life checkers adventure, you need a friend, a flat spot, a checkerboard and 24 playing pieces, 12 black and 12 white or red.

PLAYING THE GAME

Players sit opposite each other, one playing black pieces, one white. Place the board between you so that each of you has a black square in the bottom left corner. Lay out the pieces on the black squares only, as shown in the diagram.

Black always goes first. The object of the game is to move your own pieces across the board and capture or block in all of your opponent's pieces. Pieces can land only on black squares.

In one turn you can:

- move forward one square diagonally.

- capture an opponent's piece if it lies in the square diagonally ahead of you, and if diagonally beyond that is an empty square. Leap over the opponent's piece and land in the empty square. Remove the captured piece from the board.

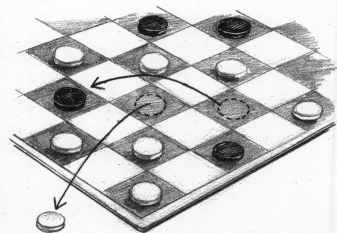

If you could capture an opponent's piece, but instead make a move that captures no pieces, your opponent has three choices before she takes her turn: she can remove your piece from the board; she can force you to replay the move and capture her piece; or she can leave the board as it is.

If you move a piece safely to the opposite side of the board, your opponent must "crown" it with one of your captured pieces. In the turns that follow, crowned pieces can move backward or forward. There may be several crowned pieces on the board at once.

- leap your piece diagonally forward and over two or more of your opponent's pieces one at a time, if your opponent's pieces are sitting so it is possible. You must be able to land in an empty square beyond each piece. Take all captured pieces off the board.

NO BOARD? NO PIECES?

You don't need a store-bought checkerboard and official pieces to play this game. You can scratch a "board" into the dirt or draw one on a flat rock with chalk and use colored bottle caps or flat pebbles for pieces. Divide the playing surface into 64 squares, 8 across and 8 down. To give the idea of light and dark squares, color or scratch in every alternate square.

The first checkers game 1000 years ago was probably improvised too, using pieces from a game called backgammon on a chessboard scratched in the dirt.

FIVES AND ONES

Are you lucky at dice? There are big points to be won in this game. You'll need three dice raided from other games, a pen and a piece of paper, and at least two players. The first one to 5000 wins. Here's hoping your luck holds!

SCORING

- = 50 points

- 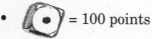 = 100 points

- three of a kind are worth the sum of the three dice multiplied by 100, for example

 x 100

= 1200 points

- If you roll 2, 3, and 4 together you lose 100 points. There are no negative scores, so if your score was 50, your new score is 0.

= −100 points

PLAYING THE GAME

1.

Each player rolls one die. The highest roll goes first.

2.

Before you can get on the scoreboard, you must roll at least 300 points in three rolls, for example:

First roll = 50 points

Second roll = 100 points

Third roll = 150 points

Total = 300 points

3.

Once a player has reached 300, he can either put his points on the scoreboard and end his turn or throw again, trying to gain more points. If he rolls and fails, his turn is over and on his next turn he must start all over again.

4.

If a player fails to score 300 points in three rolls, the next player tries her luck.

5.

Once a player is on the board, he may roll as many times as he wants in his turn, as long as a 5, 1 or three of a kind are rolled. The player can end his turn anytime and add his points to the board. If he fails to roll a 5, 1 or three of a kind, he loses the points gained on that turn and his turn is over. Tip: it's better to quit while you're ahead.

6.

If a player rolls a 2, 3 and 4 her turn is over and she loses all the points acquired during that turn, as well as 100 points.

7.

When a player reaches 5000, the other player or players have one more turn to try to beat him.

MARBLES

When you play marbles, you "play for keeps." That's marble talk for winning any marble you hit — and losing your own when you miss. So, if you don't want to lose your marbles, practice these games first alone or with a friend. Head for a patch of smooth, hard dirt.

HOW TO SHOOT A MARBLE

1.
Kneel on one or both knees.

2.
Turn your hand on its side and touch the ground with at least one knuckle.

3.
Curl your index finger and balance the shooter in the curl.

4.
Brace your thumb behind the shooter, aim and then flick the shooter with your thumb, keeping the rest of your hand still.

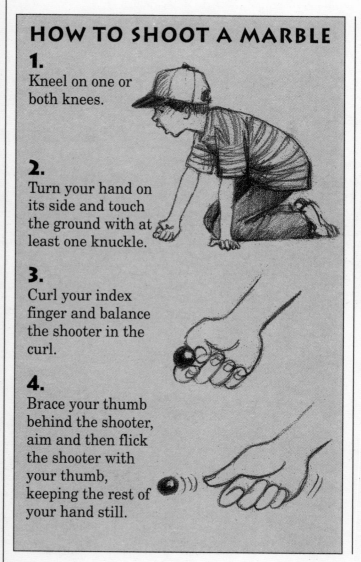

RINGER

Draw a circle about 1 m (3 ft.) in diameter in the dirt. Each player places an equal number of marbles inside the ring.

Players take turns shooting at the marbles from outside the ring. If you knock a marble out of the ring, you keep it and shoot again from where your shooter stopped. Your turn ends when you fail to knock any marbles out or your shooter stops inside the ring. Any shooters inside the ring remain there for others to shoot at. The game ends when all the marbles have been shot out of the circle.

CASTLES

Two players kneel facing each other, at least 1 m (3 ft.) apart. Each player builds a castle of four marbles — three on the bottom touching one another and one balanced on top. Both players take turns shooting at each other's castles. If one person knocks down the other's castle, that person gets to take all four castle marbles. Castle owners may keep any shooters that miss their castle. The game ends when one player has had enough.

SPANNIES

Draw a shooting line in the dirt. The first player, or the starter, rolls a marble from the shooting line. This is the target marble. The other player tries to hit that marble from the shooting line with four marbles — or some other number agreed upon at the start.

The starter wins any marble that does not hit or fall within a span of the target marble. A span is the distance from the end of the starter's thumb to the tip of his index finger. If the shooter's marble hits the target marble or comes within a span of it, she gets the target marble and her shooter. The starter then rolls a new target marble. The game is over when both players have had an equal number of turns being the starter.

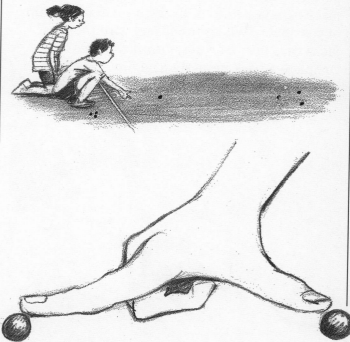

65

JACKS

Gather a group of friends together for a game of jacks. All you need is a set of five jacks, a small bouncy ball and a flat, hard surface. Learn each trick, progressing from easy to difficult. Once you've mastered the basics, challenge your friends with your own variations.

PLAYING THE GAME

Before beginning, players agree on which tricks they will attempt and in what order. Decide who goes first by taking turns throwing all five jacks up in the air and catching as many as possible on the back of your hand. Then toss the caught jacks up again and try to catch them in the cup of your palm. Whoever ends up with the most jacks goes first. She plays until she fails to complete a trick properly. The first person to complete all the tricks is the winner.

ONES

Throw the jacks on the ground. Using one hand, toss the ball into the air, pick up one jack and catch the ball after the first bounce. Transfer the jack to the other hand and repeat until all five are picked up. You are out if you drop a jack or touch one that you are not attempting to pick up.

TWOS, THREES, FOURS AND FIVES

Played as in Ones, jacks are picked up two, three, four and finally five at a time. In each trick the jacks are picked up in batches. For example in Twos, two groups of two jacks are picked up, followed by the remaining one; in Threes, three jacks are picked up together and then the remaining two.

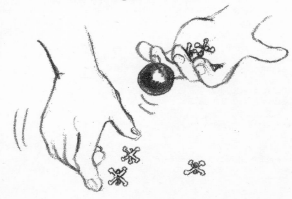

CRACK THE EGG

Throw the jacks on the ground. Toss the ball in the air, pick up one jack, tap it on the ground "cracking the egg," and catch the ball after the first bounce. Continue until all five have been picked up. Now play as in Twos, tapping the jack twice, then play as in Threes, tapping three times and so on. Did you drop any jacks? If so, you're out.

HOMEMADE JACKS

If you have a small bouncy ball but no jacks, you can substitute five small objects, such as pebbles or acorns.

WHEN JACKS WERE BONES

The game's the same, but the name's changed. Ancient Greeks threw the knucklebones of sheep on the ground, "read" them and predicted future events. In the 13th century, during the Trojan War, the Greek leader Palamedes and his soldiers played a game using knucklebones. Bone games have been popular for centuries in Asia, Polynesia, Russia and across the Arctic. Kids in Pompeii played them almost 2000 years ago!

PAPER AND PENCIL GAMES FOR TWO

Here are a few quick games to play when you have to wait around while someone buys hot dog buns or someone else looks for a dry towel. To pass the time, you need little more than a pencil, some paper and a friend.

XOXOXOXOXOXOXOXOXOXOXOXOXOXOXOXOXO

TICKTACKTOE

This simple but fascinating game was played by workmen in ancient Egypt — probably while they waited for others to get their act together too!

Draw four straight lines on a scrap of paper to form nine squares as shown. The first player writes an X in any square and the second writes an O in any other square. Players continue to enter their X or O, trying to form a row of three across, up and down, or diagonally. The first person to form a row wins. The loser (or if it's a tie, the player who went second) starts the next round.

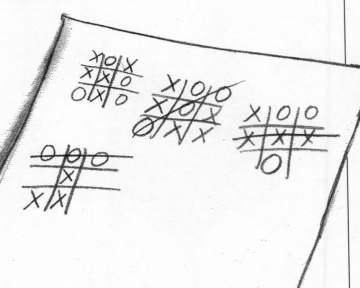

TIPS

- If you go first, place your X or O in one corner — and try to fill more corners in your next two turns.

- If you go second, you may not win unless your opponent makes a mistake. Block all the rows your opponent starts and aim for a tie.

HANGMAN

1.

Two players agree on a category, like expressions, songs or movies. If they choose expressions, for instance, the first player draws a short line on a piece of paper to represent each letter in an expression, leaving spaces between the words. The first player is the hangman and also draws a gallows on the paper.

2.

The second player names a letter she thinks may be in the expression. If her guess is correct, the hangman writes that letter at each place it occurs in the expression.

3.

The second player guesses another letter and another, trying to fill in all the letters.

4.

When the second player names a letter that is not in the expression, the hangman draws a head on the gallows. For each successive incorrect guess, he draws the body, an arm or a leg.

5.

The second player keeps guessing until she has found all the letters in the phrase or until the stick person on the gallows is complete, with a head, a body, two arms and two legs.

6.

Then it's the second player's turn to think of a expression and be the hangman.

R A _ _ T H E _ E T _ H _ P

O D R I N

MORE

TIPS

- Guess the most common letters first: E, A, O, I, D, N, P, R, S, T, L.

- When you've guessed a few letters, try to guess the whole saying before choosing another letter.

69

SHUT THE BOX

This game needs two dice, a pencil and a sheet of paper. Draw nine squares and number them 1 to 9.

The first player rolls the dice and adds up the dots. The player crosses out one, two or three squares whose numbers add up to the dice total. For instance, if 6 and 3 are thrown, the player can cross off the 9 alone, or 1 and 8, or 6 and 1 and 2, and so on. The player continues throwing the dice, trying to cross off the remaining squares.

After squares 7, 8 and 9 are crossed out, he can choose to throw only one die. When he throws a total that cannot be made with the remaining squares, his turn is over. He now adds up the unused squares to find his score. Then the second player takes her turn. The winner is the person with the lowest score.

CONNECTIONS

This game requires a pencil and a piece of graph paper. Count out an area 20 squares across and down and mark a dot at each line crossing. If you don't have graph paper, use blank paper and create a neat square of dots.

The first player draws a line to connect two adjacent dots horizontally or vertically but not diagonally. Opponents take turns connecting two dots. Every time a player closes a square, she gets to put her initial in the square and take an extra turn. The object of the game is to have your initial in the most squares by the time all the dots are connected.

TIPS

- Try not to draw a line so that you leave three sides of a square. Your opponent will get to close that square and take another turn.

- Watch for a chance to close a square in such a way that it leaves another square you can close on your extra turn — and on and on for several extra turns.

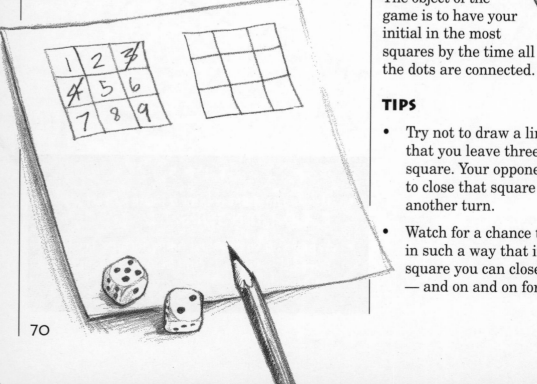

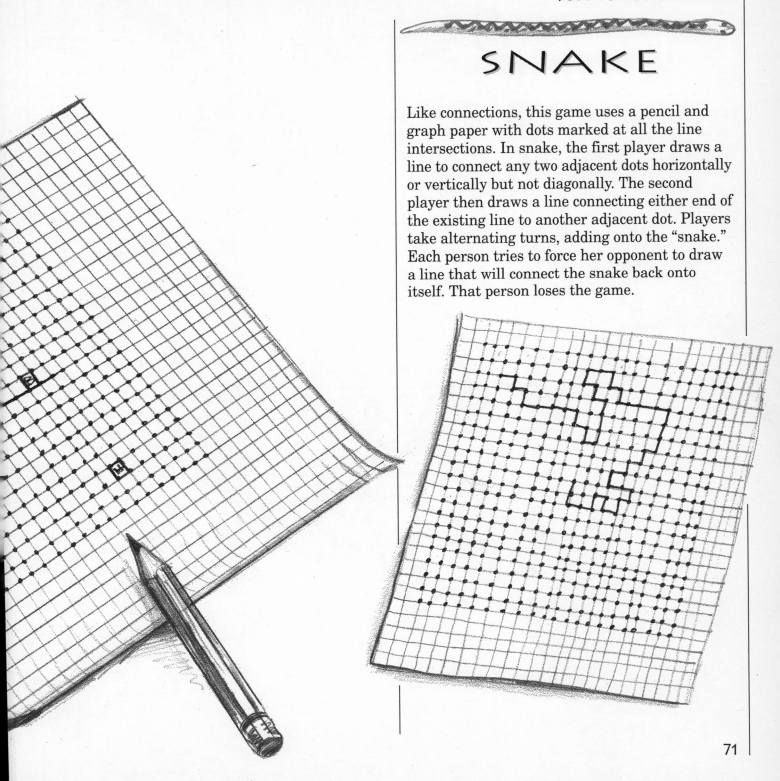

SNAKE

Like connections, this game uses a pencil and graph paper with dots marked at all the line intersections. In snake, the first player draws a line to connect any two adjacent dots horizontally or vertically but not diagonally. The second player then draws a line connecting either end of the existing line to another adjacent dot. Players take alternating turns, adding onto the "snake." Each person tries to force her opponent to draw a line that will connect the snake back onto itself. That person loses the game.

INDOOR GAMES

The games don't have to stop when the sun disappears and you move indoors. Enjoy hilarious evenings and fun-filled, rainy afternoons with the games described in this section. Act out a charade, learn to play hearts or call a friend's bluff and win the poker pot. When the sun comes out again, just carry these games outdoors and let the fun continue.

CHARADES

Your team waits on one side of the room while the other team huddles. Someone breaks from the huddle and passes you a slip of paper. It says, "I Know an Old Lady Who Swallowed a Fly." Take a deep breath and think fast — you are in for a crazy time!

PLAYING THE GAME

At the beginning of charades, each team of at least three people writes down a word or phrase for each member of the other team to act out. A phrase is handed to a player just before her turn, and teams take turns throughout the game.

When you receive your phrase, you have three minutes to get your own team to say it out loud. You cannot speak, make any noise, use props or show the paper. You have to act it out, letting your teammates know when they are right, wrong or getting close — without opening your mouth once!

Then you get to watch someone on the other team act out a crazy phrase of your team's choice — and try to better your time.

BASIC CHARADE SIGNALS

right guess
nod and point to the person who says it

wrong guess
shake your head

getting close
wave hands toward yourself, nod and smile

number of words
hold up that number of fingers

which word?
after total, hold up one finger to indicate first word, and so on

syllables
press that number of fingers on opposite forearm

which syllable?
after total, press one finger to indicate first syllable, and so on

sounds like
cup ear or pull earlobe, then act out rhyming word

little word
hold thumb and index finger close together (of, the, a, etc.)

past tense
wave hand back over shoulder

CATEGORIES

Act out one of these signals to let your team know what sort of phrase they should guess.

book title
hold your hands to look like an open book

song title
look up, open your mouth and pretend to sing

movie
hold one hand to your eye and rotate the other like a film reel

TV show
draw a box with both hands

a name
point on shirt to where a name tag would go

a place
point to the ground, away from you

a saying
hands in the air, indicate quotation marks by bending index and middle fingers

ACTING OUT "I KNOW AN OLD LADY WHO SWALLOWED A FLY"

1.
Indicate category — song title — and nod for correct answer.

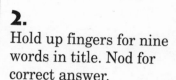

2.
Hold up fingers for nine words in title. Nod for correct answer.

3.
Try acting out whole phrase – old woman hobbling along, swallowing a fly, dying. First, let your team know you are acting out the whole thing by making a large circle, like the whole world, with your hands.

4.
If no one guesses, act out each word or phrase (*old lady, fly, swallow*)

Encourage your team to take guesses by using the "getting close" signal.

DEFINITIONS

Are appurtenances the name for life-jacket clips or noises that interrupt a storyteller? Or could they be the bubbling sounds made when an inboard motor starts? What appurtenances really are is just one part of this game. All you need to play is a group of five or more friends, one dictionary, pencils and lots of slips of paper.

PLAYING THE GAME

1.

Players sit in a loose circle or around a table.

2.

The first player flips through the dictionary to find an unfamiliar word. He spells the word out loud and reads the proper pronunciation but not the definition.

3.

Everyone invents a definition for the word and writes it on a scrap of paper. The player who chose the word writes the real definition on his slip of paper.

4.

Players pass their slips of paper to the first player, who mixes them together so no one can tell who wrote which definition.

5.

The first player then reads all the definitions aloud, one at a time, as everyone listens. It's really important to read all the definitions in the same tone of voice — no making faces or laughing.

6.

The other players, in order around the circle, say which definition they think is the real one.

7.

When the voting is over, the first player tells everyone the real definition and the points are tallied. The dictionary is passed to the left and the next player chooses a word.

SCORING

- Players get a point for every person they fool into voting for their invented definition.

- Players get two points if the definition they vote for is the real one.

- The player who selects the dictionary word gets three points if no one guesses the real definition.

The winner is the person who has the highest number of points when everyone has had the same number of turns selecting a word from the dictionary.

CHOOSING WORDS

When it's your turn to choose a word, you can find one that sounds like or suggests your summer holiday activities. Look up words like camping, sailing and swimming in a thesaurus. You'll find unusual words like bivouacking, inglenook, balneal, aquacade and gunkholing. Then look those words up in the dictionary for the definition.

PICTURE IT

How are your drawing skills? Whether you are a clever artist or not doesn't really matter. You'll need only a pencil, big pieces and small slips of paper, and a good imagination to play this word-drawing game.

PLAYING THE GAME

Divide into two teams. Each team thinks up some expressions, such as "marshmallow roast," and writes each of these on a slip of paper. There should be one expression for every member of the opposite team. If the teams are made up of different age groups, choose easier expressions for the younger kids.

One player at a time is given a slip of paper by the opposing team. When it's your turn, read what's on the paper to yourself, then put it away. On a big piece of paper, draw pictures to make your team say the expression out loud. You are not allowed to print letters or numbers or act anything out. Your teammates can ask questions, but you can only answer by drawing pictures. You have three minutes to get your team to identify the expression. Then a player on the opposite team tries to illustrate a different expression.

TIPS

- When another team member is drawing, you need to concentrate. Make lots of good guesses about what the drawings might mean.

- If a team member who is drawing seems stuck, ask helpful questions such as, "What kind of expression is it?" Then your teammate can draw a TV screen to mean a TV show title, a person singing to indicate a song title, and so on. See the Categories section in Charades (pages 74–75) for other ideas.

- Work out team symbols for "yes," "no" and "you're getting warm." You may also need a drawing symbol for numbers.

- When you are writing down expressions for the other team, remember that including a lot of nouns, or naming words, makes a definition easier. Verbs and adverbs, which describe actions, make them harder.

SOME SUMMERY EXPRESSIONS

- last one in is a dirty rotten egg!
- everyone out of the pool!
- it's hot outside
- skinny dip
- "Fire's Burning"
- "If You're Happy and You Know It, Clap Your Hands"

DOMINOES

A domino tile is like two dice that have been rolled and then attached side by side to form a rectangle. In fact that may be how dominoes were invented. Most sets are for two to four players and have 28 tiles, the highest tile being a double 6 — six dots on each end of the tile. You may, however, have a larger set that goes to double 9 or even double 12. The larger the set, the more people can play.

PLAYING DOMINOES

1.
Players place all the tiles on a flat surface facedown and shuffle them around.

2.
Each player turns up one tile, and the person whose tile has the highest number starts. The player on the left of the starter will go second, the next left third, and so on.

3.
Return the tiles to the center and reshuffle. If two people are playing, they each select seven

tiles. With three or four players, each person selects five tiles. Stand the selected tiles on their sides so no one else can see them. All remaining tiles are pushed aside and may or may not be used, depending on the game.

Some tiles have a blank at one end. The blank end is wild. The player who uses one decides the value of the blank end and it keeps that value.

THE BLOCK GAME

The first player puts any tile down on the table. The second person must play a tile that has an end that matches either end of the first tile played.

The second tile is placed matching end to matching end with the first tile in a straight line. If the second player has no matching tile to play, she loses her turn and the next person tries. The game continues until no one is able to add a tile to either end of the line.

When a player has played all her tiles, she wins. When no one can put down any more tiles and the game is blocked, the person with the lowest total number of dots on her remaining tiles wins the round. The winner adds her dot count (if she has one) to everyone else's and that total becomes her score for the round. Games are usually played to 121.

DOMINO!

MORE

THE DOMINO EFFECT

Stand up a set of dominoes in a line. Each one is placed on its end, close enough to the next domino so that when any one is knocked over, it will knock over the one behind it. Then, tap the domino at the end of the line and watch them all topple over, one after another.

BLIND HUGHIE

Each player selects five tiles without looking at them and places the tiles facedown in a row in front of him.

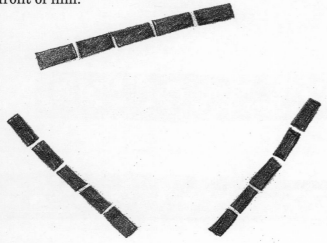

The first player picks up the tile at the left end of his row and places it in the center of the playing area.

The next player picks up the tile at the left end of her row and, if one end of it matches one end of the tile in the center, she plays it. Otherwise, the tile is placed faceup at the right-hand end of her line of dominoes.

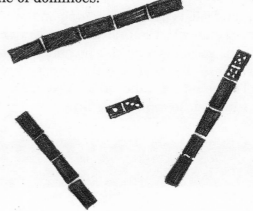

Play continues around the group, each person playing his left-hand tile or placing it back in line at the right. The first player to play all his tiles, or the player with the lowest dot count when the game is blocked, wins the round.

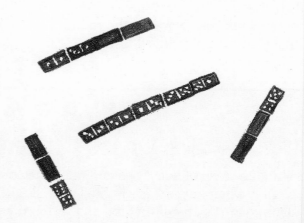

MATADOR

In this game, tiles are played not to create matching pairs but to add up to 7. The tiles that add up to 7 themselves (4:3, 5:2, 6:1) as well as 0:0 tiles are called matadors. Matadors are like wild cards, and they are the only tiles that can be played on a blank. A matador is always played sideways.

1.

The first player puts down her highest double tile or, if she has no double, her highest tile.

2.

The second player adds a tile to either end of the original domino so that the total number of dots on the halves that are touching is 7.

3.

If she does not have such a tile, she can play a matador. If she has no matador or doesn't wish to play one, she draws from the unselected tiles until she gets a tile she can use.

4.

When there are only two unselected tiles left, a player may pass or draw one of the last tiles. The winner is the first player to use up all her tiles.

5.

If no one can add a tile to the game, it is blocked. The winner is the player with the lowest number of dots on her unplayed tiles. The winner of a round scores the total of the dots on the tiles still held by her opponents.

6.

Rounds continue until a player reaches 200 points.

If you play with a set of dominoes that goes up to double 9, tiles are placed end to end to add up to 10, and a matador tile is 0:0 or one that adds up to 10 itself (9:1, 8:2, 7:3, 6:4 and 5:5).

SIMPLE CARD GAMES

If you're just learning to play cards or have a young opponent, try one of these card games. They may be simple, but they're quick-paced and good fun.

FISH

You'll get hooked on this game. All you need is a deck of 52 cards and two to five players.

PLAYING THE GAME

1.
Choose someone to deal out seven cards per player. Place the remaining cards, the draw pile, facedown on the table.

2.
Match up any pairs (two cards of the same value) in your hand and put them aside on the table in a pair pile, facedown.

3.
The dealer goes first and asks any player for a card he needs. For example, he might say "Susan, do you have an ace?" If she has the card, she must give it to him.

4.
He can continue to ask any player for cards until someone doesn't have the card he needs. That player then says, "Go fish!"

5.
The dealer takes the top card from the draw pile. If he draws the card he asked for, he says, "Got what I wanted," places the pair in his pair pile and draws again.

6.
The person to his left goes next.

7.
The object of the game is to have the most pairs when all the cards have been paired.

FISH II

Make the game more complicated by collecting four of a kind instead of pairs. This takes longer and there will be more squawks and yells as players have to part with one, two or even three cards at once.

CONCENTRATION

Play this game with one or more friends and see who has the best memory. You'll need a deck of 52 cards and a large flat surface.

PLAYING THE GAME

1.
Shuffle the cards.

2.
Lay the cards facedown, one at a time, on the table — in rows or placed randomly.

3.
Take turns turning over two cards, trying to find pairs. Color or suit doesn't matter.

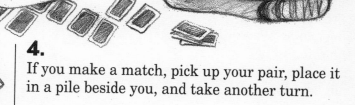

4.
If you make a match, pick up your pair, place it in a pile beside you, and take another turn.

5.
When all the cards have been matched, count up your pairs. The player with the most pairs wins.

FIFTY-TWO PICKUP

Not to be confused with concentration, fifty-two pickup is a trick, not a game. Ask someone if he wants to play fifty-two pickup. If he says yes, drop a deck of cards on the ground. Then say, "There you go, fifty-two pickup!"

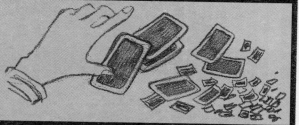

CRAZY EIGHTS

When eights are wild, anything can happen. Learn to drive your opponents crazy by playing the right card at the right time. Never play during nap time, you won't be able to keep the noise level down. Crazy eights requires a deck of 52 cards and two to four players. If more people want to play, shuffle two decks together.

PLAYING THE GAME

1.

Shuffle the deck, then choose a dealer, who deals out seven cards per player. The dealer places the remaining cards, the draw pile, facedown on the table.

2.

Sort your cards according to suits. Put any 8s to one side of your hand.

3.

The dealer creates a discard pile by placing the top card from the draw pile faceup on the table. This card determines the suit to be played. If the card is an 8, the dealer decides what suit he wants it to be.

4.

The dealer goes first by playing a card faceup on the discard pile. The card can be any card of the same suit, a card of another suit but of the same numerical value, or an 8. If the dealer has no cards that can be played, he takes the top card from the draw pile, adds it to his hand, and the person to his left takes a turn.

5.

A player can play an 8 on any turn (except as his last card) and change the suit to whatever he likes. The object of the game is to be the first person to play all the cards from your hand.

6.

When a player has one card remaining in her hand, she must say out loud, "last card." This gives the other players the opportunity to change the suit to try to prevent her from winning. If she forgets to say "last card," she must miss a turn before she can play her last card.

LAST CARD!

CRAZIER EIGHTS

Drive your friends mad with this version of Crazy Eights in which ordinary cards assume new powers. Here's a list of special cards and how they work to your advantage. Or create your own.

When you play this card		The next player must
queen of spades		draw five cards
a 2		draw two
another 2 played on the first		draw four
another 2 played on the second		draw six
another 2 played on the others		draw eight
a jack		draw one and miss a turn
a 4		miss a turn

CHEAT

For once, you're allowed to cheat all you want. That's the name and the point of this game. However, if you get caught, you'll discover that cheaters never prosper. For a rousing game of cheat, you'll need a deck of 52 cards and two to five players. With a larger crowd, mix two decks together.

PLAYING THE GAME

1.

Deal out all the cards, one at a time, in a clockwise direction.

2.

Players sort their cards by face value, regardless of suit, starting with aces and 2s, through kings.

3.

The dealer goes first, playing one or more cards facedown and declaring out loud the number of aces she is playing.

4.

If any of the other players suspect that there are more or fewer or even no aces on the table, they shout "Cheat!" The dealer must then turn over the cards she laid down to prove that they are as she declared. If the dealer did not cheat, the person who called cheat must take the cards. If the dealer is caught cheating, she takes the cards back into her hand.

5.

The play then moves in a clockwise direction, the next person laying down 2s, the next 3s and so on around the table.

6.

When "cheat" is called, the player who picks up the cards must take all the cards that are on the table, not just the last ones played.

7.

The winner is the first person to lay down all her cards.

TIPS

- Your face can help you play this game. Try to keep a straight face and declare your cards in a confident voice. Trick your opponents by looking guilty when you're innocent.

- The hand is quicker than the eye. Make your moves swiftly. By playing your cards right, you can sneak in extra cards without your opponents noticing.

3 NINES!

CAUGHT CHEATING

Cheating at cards is one thing, but when sports heroes cheat, their fans feel disappointed and betrayed. And the media doesn't let anyone forget.

- Ben Johnson of Canada was stripped of his Olympic gold medal for using illegal steroids in the 1988 Seoul Olympics.

- Craig Nettles, a New York Yankees baseball player, was called out for using an illegally weighted bat. When he hit the baseball, the bat exploded and out popped six rubber balls.

- In the 1919 World Series, eight Chicago White Sox players agreed to lose two games deliberately in exchange for $80,000 each from a gambling syndicate. They were caught and banned for life from baseball.

HEARTS

Be prepared to give your hearts away or try to "shoot the moon" and grab all the hearts for yourself. Hearts is played with a deck of 52 cards and three to six people.

PLAYING THE GAME

The object of the game is to have the lowest score. Each heart counts as 1 point and the queen of spades counts as 13.

1.

Deal out a standard deck of 52 cards one at a time, clockwise, so that each player gets an equal number of cards.

2.

If there are any cards left over, they are placed facedown in a "kitty." The kitty goes to the person who wins the first round, or trick.

3.

Players sort their cards according to suits. Aces are high, 2s are low.

4.

Each player selects three cards from her hand to pass to her neighbor on the left. You may want to rid your hand of high hearts. Players who hold the ace, king and queen will most likely take heart tricks and therefore get points against them. Or you may want to give away cards that will leave you with none of one suit. This is called a void. When this suit is led, you can sluff off, or get rid of, a heart.

5.

The person with the 2 of clubs goes first, laying the card faceup on the table. If no one has the 2 of clubs, the 3 of clubs starts.

6.

Each player, in turn, adds a card of the same suit. If a player is void in clubs, he can play any other card, including a heart or the queen of spades. The person who plays the highest card, clubs in this case, wins the trick and sets the cards aside in his pile. This player lays down first, or leads, any card to start the next trick.

7.

Play continues until all the cards have been played.

8.

Players add up their points. When someone reaches 50 points, the game is over. The person with the lowest score is the overall winner.

SHOOT THE MOON

In most hands, players try to avoid getting any hearts or the queen of spades. However, if you are dealt a hand with many high-valued hearts (ace, king and so on) plus the queen of spades, you may choose to "shoot the moon." This means getting all 13 hearts and the queen of spades. If you are successful, you score –26. If you are missing one or more of the 14 required cards, you lose — big time!

MORE

91

HEARTS FOR TWO

1.
Shuffle, cut and deal each player 13 cards. Place the remaining deck facedown on the table. This forms the draw pile.

2.
The person holding the lowest club goes first, and tricks are taken as in hearts. After each trick, players take a card from the draw pile, with the person who took the trick drawing first. This person leads for the next trick.

3.
Play continues until all cards have been played. Tally the score as in hearts. The first person to score 50 points loses.

DOMINO HEARTS

In domino hearts, the cards are worth the same value as in regular hearts, but the game is played a little differently.

PLAYING THE GAME

1.
Deal six cards to each player.

2.
Place the remaining cards facedown to form the draw pile.

3.
The person with the lowest club goes first. If a player cannot follow suit, she picks up from the draw pile until she can.

4.
She plays this card and keeps all drawn cards of other suits to play later.

5.
When the draw pile is all gone, a player who can't follow suit may discard any card she wishes, as in regular hearts.

6.
When a player has played all her cards, she is out of the game.

7.
Play continues until there is one player left. She receives a penalty point for all hearts in the tricks she has taken as well as a point for each heart left in her hand. The other players receive no points against them for this round.

8.
Rounds continue until someone reaches 31 points. The winner is the person with the lowest points.

CARDS THROUGH THE AGES

The origin of cards has been traced to the 7th century. Chinese people painted the wooden shafts of arrows with symbols, resembling those on today's cards. We think that these sticks were used to tell fortunes and for gambling. Paper cards were in general use in 14th century Germany, but the four suits on these German cards were hearts, bells, leaves and acorns. Hearts, clubs, spades and diamonds appeared on French cards during the 16th century. Around this time, cards crossed the Atlantic with American colonists.

ODD ONE OUT

In this easy card game, you try to get the other players to choose the only unpaired card in the deck. Everyone wins except the odd one out. You need two or more players and a deck of cards with one queen removed.

PLAYING THE GAME

1.

One card at a time is dealt to all the players as far as the cards go. Some players may have one more than the others.

2.

Players sort through their hands and set aside all pairs facedown on the table. If a player has three of a kind, only two go down as a pair and the third remains in his hand.

3.

All unpaired cards are held up so no one can see them except the player holding them.

4.

The player to the dealer's left chooses one card blindly from the dealer's hand. If it makes a pair with a card in her hand, she sets aside that pair. If it doesn't make a pair, she shuffles it into her hand.

5.

Then she offers her hand to the person on her left to choose a card. Play proceeds around the circle.

6.

As each player's last card is taken or put down in a pair, he goes out. The one left with the single queen loses.

TIPS

• Look at your friends' faces. If someone looks worried, chances are that he is holding a single queen. If another player chooses the single queen, that look will move on with the card. If you have to choose a card from someone's hand who seems worried, choose from the sides. Players usually stick the single queen in the middle because that's where most people choose a card from.

• If you are holding the queen, try not to look concerned. Put her in the middle of your hand. You can even look relieved and excited if a person does not choose the queen, just to fool everyone.

SLAPJACK

Get pumped up with this fast-paced game. Shuffle together several old decks, they don't need to be complete, and play with two or more people of any age. Just remember to slap gently. A quick hand beats a heavy one, hands down.

PLAYING THE GAME

1.
Deal out all the cards in a clockwise direction. The cards are left facedown in a pile in front of each player.

2.
All players watch like hawks as the person to the left of the dealer takes the top card from his pile and places it faceup in the center of the table.

3.
If the card turned up is a jack, everyone tries to be the first to slap the card. The person whose hand hits the jack first gets the card and adds it to the bottom of her pile.

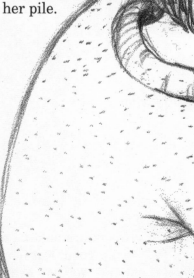

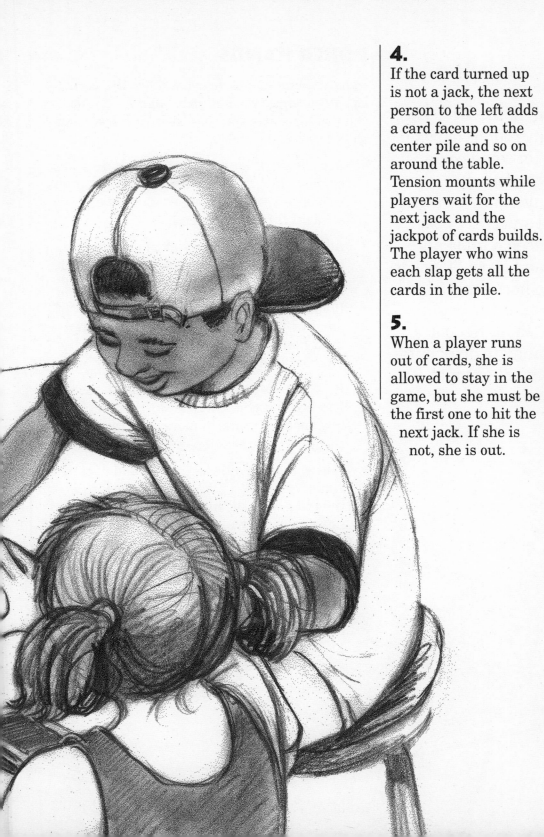

4.

If the card turned up is not a jack, the next person to the left adds a card faceup on the center pile and so on around the table. Tension mounts while players wait for the next jack and the jackpot of cards builds. The player who wins each slap gets all the cards in the pile.

5.

When a player runs out of cards, she is allowed to stay in the game, but she must be the first one to hit the next jack. If she is not, she is out.

6.

If a player makes a mistake and hits the center pile when it's not a jack, she gives the top card from her pile to the player whose card she hit.

7.

The game is over when one person has won all the cards. If this takes too long, the player with the most cards after 30 minutes wins.

WHOSE HAND HIT FIRST?

If two or more players claim to be first to the jack, check the stack of hands. Whoever's hand is on the jack at the bottom of the pile gets the jackpot.

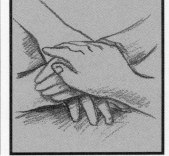

POKER

Capture the excitement of the Wild West by playing a few friendly rounds of poker. These first pages explain some poker basics. Turn the pages to find rules for specific poker games, including straight poker, spit in the ocean and crazy poker.

To play poker, you need a table and chairs, a deck of cards and about 30 poker chips per player (for a short game). If you don't have poker chips, use counters such as peanuts in the shell. Keep a jarful of poker chips handy to distribute at the beginning of each poker night, and collect them all again at the end of the evening.

POKER HANDS

In most poker games your hand has five cards. In games where you get more than five cards, you usually select your best five for the scoring showdown at the end.

- Ace is high, then king, queen, jack, 10 and so on down to 2. (Ace can be low, but only in the sequence 5, 4, 3, 2, A — see straight and straight flush, next page.)

- All suits are equal — a jack of diamonds is tied with the jack of hearts, jack of clubs or jack of spades, but is greater than any 10.

- If you're very lucky, all the cards in your hand will fit a pattern (see next page), but most hands have some cards that fit and others that don't.

- If two hands have the same pattern, the hand with higher cards is worth more. So two queens are worth more than two 10s, though they are both pairs.

- Where there is a tie in pattern and in card value — say both players have two kings — the hand with the highest card that doesn't fit the pattern wins. If those cards have the same value, the next highest breaks the tie.

These diagrams show the value or rank of poker hands from the lowest to the highest:

1. **High card**
   The least valuable hand has five unmatched cards.

2. **A pair**
   Two cards of the same rank and three other cards.

3. **Two pairs**
   Two cards of one rank, two of another and one other card.

4. **Three of a kind**
   Three cards of the same rank and two other cards.

5. **Straight**
   A sequence of five cards in more than one suit.

6. **Flush**
   Five cards in the same suit.

7. **Full house**
   Three cards of one rank and two of another.

8. **Four of a kind**
   Four cards of the same rank plus one other card.

9. **Straight flush**
   A sequence of five cards in the same suit.

10. **Royal flush**
    A straight flush of the highest cards.

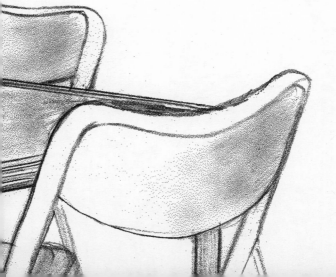

MORE

THE DEAL

Players sit around a table. Any player deals the cards faceup until one person gets a jack. That person will deal the first hand. From then on, the deal passes to the player on the dealer's left.

The cards should be shuffled several times by the dealer. The player to the dealer's right can cut the deck if he wishes after the shuffle. Players ante (see Betting). The dealer deals the cards facedown around the table, starting with the player to her left and ending with herself, until each player has the right number of cards for the game.

People play many variations of poker. It's a good idea to review the rules at the beginning so you're all playing the same game!

BETTING

Betting in poker is like saying you think your hand is better than anyone else's. Players bet by putting chips in the "pot," a place in the center of the table. It's a good idea to keep bets small to keep everyone in the game longer.

1.

To join a game, players **ante** by placing one chip in the pot before the deal.

2.

After looking at her cards, the player to the dealer's left decides if she is going to **open** the betting or pass. If she passes, each player to her left, in turn, can open or pass until someone opens.

3.

The player who opens adds a chip to the pot and announces, "I'll bet one chip." After that, players to the left, in turn around the circle, decide if they will **stay in** by adding a chip too.

4.

Any time during the game, a player can **fold** — put his cards on the table facedown. If someone folds, he is out for that hand and loses any chips he already put in the pot.

5.

A player can **raise**, which means he adds one or two more chips to the pot. This challenges the others to equal the raised bet if they dare stay in. If they all fold instead, he wins the pot.

POKER GAMES

Get ready for a night of frontier-style poker now that you know the rules (see pages 98–101).

♠ ♥ ♦ ♣ ♠ ♥ ♦ ♣ ♠ ♥ ♦ ♣ ♠

STRAIGHT POKER

In this old poker game for two to four players, each player who antes is dealt five cards. Players look at their cards and the player to the left of the dealer must make an opening bet. The players who follow can fold, stay in or raise in one round of betting. Then, players who stay in show their cards and the best hand wins. If one player raises during the betting, and no one meets his raise, he wins and doesn't have to show his hand.

Straight poker is a game for bluffing. Players remain "poker-faced," showing no emotion, trying to outwit one another. Because no one can discard or draw new cards to improve a hand, chances are that a pair will be good enough to win.

DRAW POKER

Two to eight players can play draw poker, but it's best with six or seven. After the deal, the game follows in four parts: the opening bet, the draw, second bets and the showdown.

THE OPENING BET

Starting with the player to the dealer's left, players pass or open by putting a chip in the pot. You should have a pair of jacks or better to open, but you don't have to open even if you have a good hand. Once someone opens, each player in turn can fold, stay in or raise. Betting continues until all players have declared they are staying in or folding. If everyone drops out but the opener, she collects the pot but must show she had at least a pair of jacks to open.

THE DRAW

Players who stay in can discard up to four cards from their hands facedown and get the same number of new cards from the dealer. The dealer works clockwise around the table, one player at a time, collecting the discards and replacing them with cards from the top of the deck, facedown.

SECOND BETS

Whoever opened the first round of betting, opens the second. If the opener has folded, the next player to the left can open or pass. Betting continues until all players have chosen to fold or stay in.

THE SHOWDOWN

Everyone who is still in lays his hand faceup on the table. The player with the best poker hand wins the pot.

MORE POKER GAMES

Try your luck with these variations on the game of poker. Keep the rules handy (see pages 98–101).

FIVE-CARD STUD

Five-card stud is similar to straight poker (page 102) except that some cards are dealt faceup. This game is best with four or five players.

1.

Players ante and the dealer gives each person one card facedown. Players peek at their cards.

2.

A second card is dealt to everyone faceup. The deal stops for a round of betting. The player with the highest card showing opens, or bets first. Players may fold, stay in or raise and betting continues until everyone stays in or folds.

3.

The dealer gives each person who is still in a second card faceup. The player with the best hand showing starts another round of betting. Players stay in or fold.

4.

A third card is dealt faceup to all active players, followed by another round of betting. Then a fourth card is dealt faceup with a final round of betting among remaining players.

5.

When the betting has ended, those who are still in show their facedown card and the best poker hand wins. If all players but one fold in any round, that one player takes the pot without having to show his down card.

SPIT IN THE OCEAN

WILD! I HAVE A ROYAL FLUSH!

This game adds a wild card to draw poker. Two to seven people can play. When a card is wild, any card like it in your hand is wild. If 2s are wild, one player can call any 2 the ace of spades and another can call a 2 the jack of hearts. It can make you spitting mad!

Spit in the ocean starts as draw poker (see page 103), except that every player is dealt only four cards facedown. Then the dealer turns one card faceup on the table. That card is the fifth card for everyone's hand and it is wild. So, if you have another card of the same rank in your dealt hand, it's wild too. You have to figure out how you can best use your wild card or cards.

Follow the same steps as draw poker with a round of opening bets, a chance to discard cards and replace them (including your whole hand), second bets and the showdown. Wild cards mean a player might get five of a kind, which beats a royal flush.

CRAZY POKER

In this hilarious game, all players are dealt one card facedown. Players must not look at their own card and must hold it against their foreheads facing the other players. Looking at the other players' cards, everyone bets whether her own card is the highest or lowest. When all bets are on the table, players put their cards on the table to see who wins. This has to be the silliest game of poker.

BLACKJACK

Blackjack, or Twenty-one, is a casino gambling game where the stakes can run high. First, learn the basics of the game. All you need is one or more opponents and a deck of 52 cards. Then, if you want to add gambling to your game, check out "Playing for eats" on page 108.

THE DEALER

The traditional way to select the first dealer in blackjack is for one player to shuffle the deck and then deal the cards faceup, in a clockwise direction. The first player to receive an ace is the dealer.

The dealer shuffles the deck again and asks any player to cut. Then the dealer takes the top card, shows it to everyone and "burns" it by putting it face up on the bottom of the deck. Aces can't be burnt, so if an ace is turned up, the dealer starts over with shuffling, cutting and so on. After this ceremony, the dealer is ready to begin.

PLAYING THE GAME

The object of the game is to have cards that add up to 21 or are closest to 21 without going over. A tie goes to the dealer. Aces can be high or low, face cards are worth 10 and all other cards, their numerical value: 2 = 2, 8 = 8 and so on.

1.
One card is dealt facedown to each player in a clockwise direction. Then a second card is dealt faceup.

2.

Players peek at their turned-down card, add up the value of their two cards and decide if they'll risk taking another card.

3.

The dealer starts with the player to his left. If a player wants another card, she says, "Hit me" to the dealer, who deals another card faceup. Each player continues taking cards until she decides to "stand," or stop with the count that she has.

OK...HIT ME AGAIN !

4.

You go "bust" if your count exceeds 21. You are out of the hand and return your cards to the dealer, who places them faceup under the burnt card.

5.

Players, but not the dealer, whose two dealt cards make a pair (for example, two 3s), can play two hands at once by turning over both cards and receiving a "hit" on each card, facedown. Continue as above.

HIT ME ON BOTH.

MORE

6.

The dealer gives hits to all players in turn. Then he turns his two cards faceup and decides how many hits he wants. The hand that is closest to 21 is declared the winner.

7.

If your two cards are an ace and a face card, you've got blackjack. You are the automatic winner — unless the dealer has blackjack too.

8.

The winner of the hand deals next. The cards from the previous hand are placed faceup under the burnt card and the deal is made from the rest of the deck.

9.

Play continues until the dealer comes to the burnt card. He gathers up all the discards, shuffles and continues the hand in play.

PLAYING FOR EATS

At the beginning of the game, the dealer shells out 25 peanuts (or jube-jubes, jelly beans or other small treats) to each player. Before the dealing of each hand, players ante by placing a peanut in front of them on the table. This indicates the player is "in," or wants to play the hand. Whoever wins the hand gets the goodies people put in to play.

RUMOLI

Rumoli mixes the bluffing of poker with a keep-your-wits-about-you board game. It can last the whole evening and involve four to nine players of any age so long as they can play poker (see pages 98–101), pay attention and count.

You'll need:
a deck of cards
about 30 chips per player
a rumoli cloth. (If you don't have a rumoli cloth, draw one on an old sheet or on the back of a plastic cloth.)

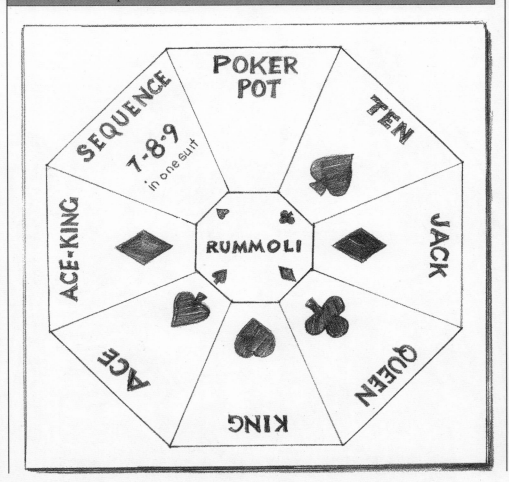

LADY LUCK

If players aren't getting good cards in poker, they try to change their luck. Some people think that can happen when it's their turn to shuffle, cut or deal the cards. Players may knock on the deck, murmur a wish, sit on a handkerchief, kiss their fingers before they touch the cards, make an unusually small or a big cut, leave one card facedown until the other cards are organized in their hands — all for better luck. One thing people *can't* do is change seats once a game has started. If a new player joins, she takes a vacant seat and the other players stay where they were.

MORE

PLAYING RUMOLI

Each player receives an equal number of chips. To start a round, players ante by putting one chip on each of the nine sections of the rumoli cloth. One player deals out all the cards, one hand per player but two hands for herself.

1.
Players pick up their hands. The dealer picks up only one of her two hands. If she doesn't like it, she can discard it and pick up her second hand. However, if she likes the first hand, she can sell the second one, sight unseen, to whichever player will give her the most chips for it. The the buyer's first hand is removed from the game.

2.
The player to the left of the dealer asks, "Are you in?" Those who want to play a round of poker (see straight poker, page 102) with the best cards in their hands place a chip in the poker pot.

If someone raises by playing two chips, other players can say, "I'll see you," and match the bet. When the betting is finished, the players who are in the game show their hands. The best poker hand takes the pot.

3.
The winner of poker then discards her lowest card. If that is a 3 of spades, the person holding the 4 of spades discards it next, then the 5, the 6 and so on until the sequence stops. Since one hand has been removed from the game, the discarding will regularly stop before a suit has run right through.

4.
When the sequence of discarding a suit stops, the last person to play gets to discard his lowest card of the other color. If he can't play one, the player on his left discards. The sequence keeps starting up until one player is out of cards and calls "rumoli." That player wins the chips on the rumoli section of the cloth.

Players give a chip to the winner for every card they still hold.

5.
During the discarding, everyone watches for the jack of diamonds, 7-8-9 of the same suit in sequence, or any other card or group of cards that has its own section on the rumoli cloth. Players can claim the chips in the section as they discard the cards.

6.
For round two, the deal moves to the player left of the first-round dealer. Rounds are repeated until everyone has had a chance to deal, someone is declared the winner, or everyone is worn out and ready for bed!

GAMES TO MAKE

There are many games you can create from stuff you may find around the house in the summertime. Make them in a quiet moment so you're ready to play when friends drop by.

When you feel like stretching your muscles, make old-fashioned basketball hoops or a comet ball, complete with tail. For quieter moments, try pickup sticks or tiddlywinks. You'll get great satisfaction knowing your fun comes from the skill of your own hands.

21 BASKETBALL

If you have a basketball but no hoops and no team, you can still play a rousing game with a friend and practice your skills.

You'll need:

an old bushel basket, wastebasket or a plastic pail big enough to hold the ball

a saw

a hammer and some nails

a piece of chalk

1.

Find a flat, hard surface, such as a patio or a driveway with a post, pole, deck or wooden fence beside it.

2.

With an adult's help and permission, saw the bottom off your old basket. (This is only necessary if the basket will be placed too high to get the ball out of easily — see next step.)

3.

Ask an adult to tack one side of your basket no more than 3 m (9 ft.) up on the post or the side of the deck or fence.

4.

With the chalk draw a line on the asphalt about 3 m (9 ft.) away from the basket. This is the free-throw line.

PLAYING THE GAME

To start, the players take turns trying to "break the ice" – that is, sink a basket from the chalk line. Once a player breaks the ice, she can start counting points and gets to shoot again and again from behind the chalk line until she misses the basket, ending her turn.

When the ice-breaker finally misses, the other player runs to get the rebound and tries to break the ice from where he catches it. If he gets a basket, he gets to try a free throw from behind the chalk line and keeps shooting and counting points until he misses. Then the first player runs for the rebound and shoots from where she grabs it.

If either player shoots an air ball — that is, shoots and misses the basket so badly the rim is not even touched — his opponent grabs the "rebound" and walks to anywhere under the basket to take a shot.

SCORING

Players earn 1 point for breaking the ice, 2 points for every other free-throw basket from the chalk line, and 1 point for every basket earned from a rebound. The first player to reach exactly 21 wins. If a player goes over 21, she goes back to 0. This can happen if a player has 20 points and then sinks a free throw.

PEACH BASKETBALL

When Canadian James Naismith invented the game of basketball in 1891, he tacked a peach basket to each end wall of a gymnasium in Massachusetts. Why peach baskets? He grew up on a fruit farm.

COMET BALL

Make a comet ball and leave your old games of catch in the dust — intergalactic dust, that is. With a comet ball you can double both the speed and the distance of your throws. Just be careful you don't throw your comet ball so high it gets caught in the top of a tall tree or breaks a neighbor's window.

You'll need:

a discarded pair of nylon stockings

scissors

an old tennis ball or a rubber ball

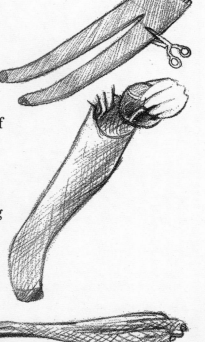

1.
Cut off one whole stocking leg with your scissors.

2.
Stuff the ball into the toe of the cutoff stocking leg.

3.
Tie a knot at the heel of the stocking so the ball won't work its way back down the leg.

4.
Find a big, open, outdoor space and practice throwing your comet ball. Hold it by the leg of the stocking and swing it around and around, then let it go. To catch the comet ball, grab for the tail (the leg of the stocking) as it flies by.

PLAYING WITH THE COMET BALL

Try playing throw and catch games, but stand far apart. Or line up and see who can throw the comet ball the farthest.

Adapt strategies for monkey in the middle. In the regular game, two players throw a ball back and forth, and a third player in the middle tries to catch it. With a comet ball, the ball will sail way over your head if you are in the middle. You have to move so you're nearly at one end or the other to have any chance of catching it. When the middle person catches the ball, he switches places with the player who threw it.

COMETS AND METEORS

Comets are clouds of frozen gas and dust particles left over from the birth of our solar system. They travel in long orbits or trails. When a comet nears the Sun, part of its icy coating melts and some dust particles fall off along the trail. The warming gases reflect sunlight, so the comet seems to grow a large head and tail.

Bright comets are seen only three or four times in a hundred years. But you can see a meteor shower each year in the month of August. Meteors actually begin as dust particles left along an old comet trail. The particles hit the edge of Earth's atmosphere and flash as they vaporize on contact. Each August, Earth passes across an ancient comet trail and we are rewarded with several meteors, or shooting stars, each hour.

HOOP AND ARROW

Can you hit a moving target? Long ago, this skill could mean the difference between having dinner or going hungry. Native North Americans invented a game to practice their throwing skills when they were relaxed and well fed. You can make this game and see how good your chances of survival would have been before the days of grocery stores.

You'll need:
a circular, plastic lid at least 15 cm (6 in.) across
scissors
a large, empty, net bag, like the kind onions come in
twist ties
a thin, branched twig
knife
Plasticine
feathers for decoration

1.
Use scissors to cut the center out of the plastic lid so that all you have left is a 1.5 cm ($^5/_8$ in.) plastic rim. This is the frame of your hoop.

2.
Slip the net bag over your hoop and cut the open end of the bag with scissors so that the netting barely extends beyond the hoop.

3.
Stretch and tighten the net bag all around the hoop and secure the bag to the hoop with twist ties. You'll have to fold and roll the edges of the open end of the net bag toward the hoop until the fold lies along the rim and then tie it down.

4.
Flatten the twist ties against the plastic rim. Your hoop should now be covered tidily with netting so that the hoop can roll smoothly on its side.

5.
With an adult's help, trim the twig down to a few branches. Cut the tip straight across cleanly with the knife. Avoid a sharp point as this can be dangerous.

6.
Roll a small ball of Plasticine and stick it on the cut end of the twig. The Plasticine ball should be much smaller than the holes in the net bag.

7.
Attach feathers to the ends of the branches on the twig with twist ties.

PLAYING THE GAME

One player rolls the hoop across the ground and the other tries to throw the arrow into it. The players take turns seeing who can put the arrow closest to the center of the net. As you improve your skills, stand farther and farther back and see how you do.

SHUTTLECOCK

The original game of badminton needed only a homemade shuttlecock and a circle of players ready to try their skills at running, twisting and jumping. Why not make a shuttlecock and play this ancient game?

You'll need:

10 to 16 small feathers of about the same length. You may have to collect them over time.

a pocketknife

a pin

a cork from a wine bottle

1.

With an adult's help, sharpen the tip of each feather shaft with the pocketknife. Be sure to cut away from your body and your legs.

2.

With the pin, prick 16 evenly spaced holes around the outside edge of the thinner end of the cork.

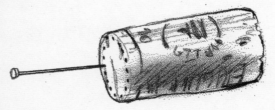

3.

Insert the sharpened end of each feather shaft into a hole and push until the feather sticks.

4.

Twist the feathers so that their edges overlap to form a ring. When tossed in the air, your shuttlecock should spiral down and then land on its featherless end.

PLAYING THE GAME

In one old Korean shuttlecock game called *chae-bi*, players formed a circle and tried to keep the shuttlecock up in the air for as long as possible using the inside edges of their feet instead of rackets. This version is like the modern game of foot tennis called hackey sack, which uses a knitted ball rather than a shuttlecock.

In an old Chinese game, players hit the shuttlecock back and forth in the air with wood and animal-skin rackets similar to Ping-Pong paddles. People said whoever kept the shuttlecock in the air for the longest would have a long life; and whoever made it fly high would reach heaven.

Whether you play the old Korean or Chinese version, you'll find that keeping the shuttlecock high takes quick moves and cooperation.

ANCIENT GAMES

Games of shuttlecock were played in Asia 2000 years ago, and playing by the ancient rules can be fun. But you may want to pass on some other ancient games, such as bull-leaping. Five thousand years ago in Crete, an athlete in this event would grab a bull by its horns, flip to stand on the bull's back and then flip again to land behind the beast.

121

MIDWAY GAMES

Practice up for your next trip to a fair playing these games of accuracy.

MUFFIN-PAN MIDWAY

Bring the excitement of the midway to your home.

You'll need:

an old 12-hole muffin pan

a permanent marker

some string

four pennies

a pen and some paper

1.
Turn the muffin pan on its side so there are four holes across and three down.

2.
Use the marker to label each hole with a number value as shown.

3.
Lean the muffin pan against a wall on a carpeted floor or on top of a towel.

4.
Mark a starting line on the floor with a piece of string 2 m (6 ft.) long. Move the string farther away from the muffin pan if the game is too easy.

PLAYING THE GAME

Players take turns kneeling behind the starting line and trying to throw pennies into the pan. Gentle underhand throws usually work best. Keep score after each turn. The first person to score 1000 wins.

TIDDLYWINKS

Be the first one to shoot all your winks into a cup and you've won the game. Sounds easy, but the winks don't always cooperate. Practice will improve your accuracy.

GETTING READY

- Each player needs four winks and a shooter. For winks, use different colored buttons, about 2 cm (3/4 in.) across, for each player. Use a larger button or a coin about 3 cm (1 in.) across as a shooter.

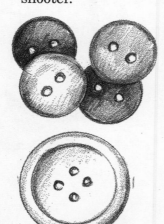

- Use a small margarine tub, measuring 3 cm (1 in.) tall, for the target cup.

- A flannel sheet, laid flat on a hard floor, makes the best tiddlywinks play area.

- Place the target cup in the middle of the sheet. Use a piece of string to mark a curved starting line, 0.5 m (1½ ft.) away from the cup.

PLAYING THE GAME

1.
Players line up their winks on the starting line.

2.
To start the game, each player takes one shot toward the cup, leaving his wink where it lands.

3.
The player whose wink is closest to the cup goes first. He takes another shot with the same wink. If his wink lands in the cup, he starts again with a second wink. If he misses the cup, his turn is over.

4.
Play continues, clockwise, until one person has all four winks in the cup. Sort out the winks and play again.

5.
When the game is over, store the winks in the margarine tub.

SHOOTING WINKS

Hold the shooter between the thumb and index finger and press the shooter down on the edge of the wink. The wink will flick away.

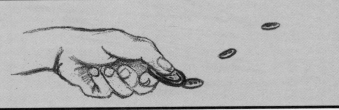

PICKUP STICKS

How steady is your hand? How sharp is your eye? Make a set of pickup sticks and challenge one or two friends to test their skills.

You'll need:
20 straight, narrow sticks with the bark peeled off, about 12 cm (4½ in.) long. Trimmed wooden barbecue skewers will also do.
acrylic paints (black, green, orange and yellow)
a paintbrush
water for cleaning the brush

- Paint both ends of one stick black.

- Paint both ends of three sticks green.

- Paint both ends of six sticks orange.

- Paint both ends of ten sticks yellow.

PLAYING THE GAME

1.
Gather up all the sticks except the black one and hold them in a bunch. Insert the black stick into the center.

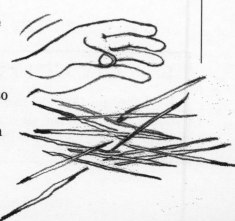

2.
Hold the sticks with one hand so that one end of the bunch touches the floor. Open your hand and pull it back quickly so the sticks topple on top of one another on the floor.

3.

Players take turns trying to pick up one stick at a time, using only their fingers and without moving any other stick.

4.

If a player picks up one stick and the others do not move, she sets the stick aside and gets another turn. The player continues as long as she is successful.

5.

If someone, in trying to pick up a stick, wiggles another, she leaves both sticks where they lie and her turn is over.

6.

The person who successfully retrieves the black stick can use it as a tool to help retrieve other sticks. The black stick is better than your finger for flicking sticks off the top of the pile or for pulling back a stick that is touching others. You still cannot wiggle others when using the black stick.

SCORING

When all the sticks have been picked up, players count their score.

- The black stick is worth 4 points.
- Each green stick is worth 3 points.
- Each orange stick is worth 2 points.
- Each yellow stick is worth 1 point.

HOMESTYLE BINGO

A large bowl of popcorn and a lineup of prizes shows you're ready to make a night of it. Bingo has so many variations, it takes a few hours to try them all. It's a great game for players of all ages.

You can make and find the equipment you'll need to play bingo without a trip to the store. If you don't have the exact supplies, improvise. Keep all the pieces in a shoe box so you'll always be ready to play.

MAKING BINGO CARDS

You'll need:
20 pieces of cardboard 10 cm x 12 cm (3³/₄ in. x 4¹/₂ in.)
a 30 cm (12 in.) ruler
a pencil
a felt marker

1.

The bingo cards are 10 cm (3³/₄ in.) across the top and the sides are 12 cm long (4¹/₂ in.) Make a pencil dot every 2 cm (³/₄ in.) across the top and bottom of the cardboard. Draw lines to connect the dots as shown.

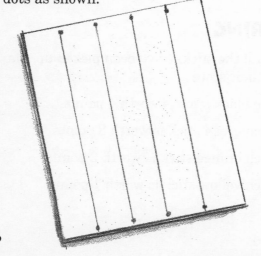

2.

Turn the card on its side and measuring from the top, make five pencil dots 2 cm (³/₄ in.) apart along both sides of the card. Draw lines to connect the dots. Each card has five squares across and six squares down.

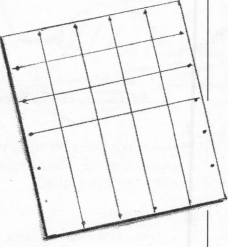

3.

Use the felt marker to print "BINGO" in the five spaces across the top of the card.

4.

Draw a star in the middle of the card, under the "N," as shown.

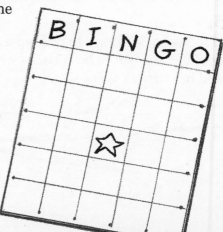

MARKING THE CARDS

The numbers 1 through 75 are used in bingo, but only certain numbers can go in the squares under each letter.

B = 1 to 15
I = 16 to 30
N = 31 to 45
G = 46 to 60
O = 61 to 75

Keeping these numbers in mind, mark each card with numbers. Make sure no two cards are the same. Here are two sample cards:

MAKING A CALLER CHART

Make a chart on which the caller can record each number that has been called. Divide a larger piece of cardboard, approximately 15 cm x 30 cm (6 in. x 12 in.), as you did for the bingo cards, but make 15 boxes below each letter. In the boxes print the numbers 1 through 75, starting with B-1 and ending with 0-75.

MORE

127

MAKING MARKERS AND CALL NUMBERS

Make the markers and call numbers out of disks of paper. If you have a huge penny collection, save paper and use them as markers.

You'll need:
four sheets of lightweight, colored construction paper
a penny
a pencil
scissors
a black felt marker
two small margarine tubs with lids

1.

Use a penny to trace as many circles as possible on a piece of construction paper. You should get about 80 circles per sheet of paper.

2.

Cut out the circles. Repeat until you have about 300 markers. To make the cutting go faster, fold your paper once or twice, then trace your circles and cut through all the layers.

3.

Label 75 of the markers from B-1 through O-75. Set these aside in a margarine tub with a lid. Put the remaining markers in the other tub.

PLAYING THE GAME

The object of bingo is to be the first player to cover your card in a certain pattern determined at the beginning of each game. Standard patterns include an X, a horizontal line, a vertical line, a diagonal line, an L-shape, the four outside edges of the card, and a full card. Take turns picking the pattern for each game. Choose a standard pattern or create your own crazy pattern. Try an H, a Z or a summer stripe — all the Bs, Ns and Os.

1.

Every player gets at least one bingo card and a handful of plain markers. Players then cover the star in the middle of each card with a marker.

2.

Without peeking, the caller pulls a call number from the margarine tub, calls out the letter and the number and places the marker on the caller card.

3.

The caller continues until someone has completed the required pattern and shouts "Bingo!" The caller double-checks his chart, making sure all the numbers covered have been called.

4.

All players clear off the markers, agree on another pattern and play again. Keep your bingo card, or trade it in for a different one.

PLAYING FOR PRIZES

Liven up the game with wild or tasty prizes. Before the bingo game, collect natural treasures such as rocks, driftwood or bird feathers. Or make prizes such as individual bags of peanuts, popcorn or rice-cereal squares. The person who decides on the pattern also determines the prize.

WATERFRONT

It's wet and wonderful down along the shore. As long as there's water, you'll have a cool time. Learn a new swimming game, rule the air mattress or play a board game in the sand. But first, review the water safety rules so each activity is safe and fun.

WATER SAFETY'S NO GAME

Water fun and water safety go hand in hand. Learn the following safety rules and make a poster to hang at home or in your boathouse.

- Always swim with a buddy. Ask an adult lifeguard to keep a head count of all swimmers.

- With the help of an adult, learn where the water is a safe depth and where it's too deep for your swimming ability.

- Swim parallel to the shore, never straight out into deep water.

- Check first, dive second. Dive only into deep water that you are familiar with. Never dive into shallow, rocky, reedy or unknown waters.

- In unfamiliar water it's safest to walk out and swim on the way back in.

- Surf's up? Check tides, waves and currents with an adult. Wait until the water is safe for swimming.

- Keep clear of boats and water-skiers.

- Use inflatable tubes and toys with care. Wind and currents can quickly carry you into deep water.

- Keep your beach clean and safe for people and wildlife. Remove any glass, cans or trash.

- Keep a reach pole, life jacket or paddle in a handy spot on the shore for rescues.

- Wear a properly fitted life jacket in boats or for deep-water games.

- Double-check for boats when swimming back to shore from a raft.

SKIN GUARD

You need more than a lifeguard by the water. Protect your skin from the sun's ultraviolet rays. Wear a sun hat and a big T-shirt over your swimsuit when you're not swimming. Ask an adult which sunscreen is right for you and if it needs reapplying after you get out of the water.

SAFELY WITHIN REACH

Practice this shore-to-water maneuver and you can rescue an adult in distress — even if you only weigh 35 kg (75 pounds). Never swim out — a frantic swimmer can pull you under.

- Call for help.

- Hold on to one end of a reach pole and lie flat on the dock or shore. Only your head, shoulders and outstretched arms should extend over the water.

- Hold out the pole to the struggling swimmer. Speak calmly and encourage the swimmer to hold on.

- Slowly pull the pole toward the dock until the swimmer reaches safety.

SWIMMING GAMES

On those hot summer days when you want to stay in the water, keep the gang cool but active with these games. All players must be able swimmers who are familiar with the depth of the water. Ask an adult to lifeguard.

SHARK

You'll need three or more players for this game.

1.
Decide on the area to be used — such as from the point to the dock or to the sandbar. You'll want an area about the size of a big swimming pool where the water is not over your head.

2.
Choose one swimmer to be the shark. The other players are bait fish.

3.
The shark counts to ten while the bait fish scatter.

4.
The shark must swim with one hand on his hip, elbow up like the fin of a shark, while he tries to tag bait fish underwater. Be careful not to kick. This shark is not out for blood!

5.
Each tagged player turns into a shark and, with her fin showing, swims after bait fish. Any bait fish swimming out of bounds becomes a shark too.

6.
The game is over when all the bait fish have been caught.

J A I L E R

You'll need three or more players for this game.

1.
Decide on boundaries as in shark. Half the game area is the jail, half is a home-free zone.

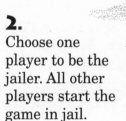

2.
Choose one player to be the jailer. All other players start the game in jail.

3.
The jailer patrols the middle of the game area, where he can stand. He walks back and forth, keeping his eyes shut.

4.
All jailed players try to swim past the jailer, without being heard. If the jailer hears someone trying to escape, he points to the player and orders her back into jail.

5.
The game is over when all players get out of jail.

WATER MAY I

When you play May I? on land, you tread lightly and mind your manners. "Stephanie, you may take two giant steps." "Mother, may I?" "Yes, you may." So polite.

In water, it's treading of a different sort, but you still have to ask permission. Get three or more friends together and play this polite game.

1.
Set the boundaries as in Jailer. The person who is It stands at one end of the swimming area. All remaining players line up at the other end.

2.
It tells each player in turn to take a specified number of strokes — such as "Adrian, you may swim four backstrokes," or "Jesse, you may swim six dog-paddles."

3.
Each player must ask, "May I?" before swimming or she goes back to the starting line. The first person who swims to It, gets to be It next.

135

WATER BALL GAMES

Get an energetic and playful group together for a good time. You'll have to refuel when the games are over. Water ball is a workout.

MONKEY IN THE MIDDLE

You'll need three players and a soft rubber or plastic ball for this game.

- All players must be aware of the depth of the water. Knee-to waist-level is perfect. Keep clear of any hazards such as rocks and reeds.

- Choose one person to be in the middle. The other two throw the ball over the middle player's head.

- The middle person jumps up and tries to catch the ball. If he is successful, he replaces the thrower.

- The middle player can try to catch the throwers off guard by splashing and yelling.

BREACH REACH

Whales use their powerful tails to breach, or propel themselves out of the water. Unfortunately, people aren't equipped with tails. It would take superhuman strength for you to breach out of deep water. But you can improve your reach by planting two feet on the bottom of the lake or pool, bending your knees and pushing off.

WATER POLO

A pickup game of water polo at the lake or pool needs an even number of players. Rules are flexible. Decide, before you start, if touching bottom and time-outs are allowed. The referee can be anyone who knows the rules and can whistle or shout "stop" and "go." Use a soft beach ball for a safe game.

PLAYING THE GAME

- Decide on a game area about the size of a big swimming pool. Mark the middle with several jug buoys. (See page 158 for making jug buoys.) Make a goal at each end with two jug buoys. If you're playing in a pool, place a marker on each side to show the middle and two at each end for the goals. The goal width should be about 2 meters (6½ ft.).

- Divide the players into two teams, each with one goalie. The teams line up at opposite ends of the swimming area. The referee whistles and throws the ball into the middle.

- Players from both teams try to get to the ball, pass it to a teammate, and score a point.

- All players except the goalie must "dribble" the ball, pushing it through the water with one hand or any other part of their body. Players can also throw one-handed passes. Only the goalie can handle the ball with two hands.

- The team with the most goals wins.

FAIR PLAY

Keep the game friendly — that means no kicking, splashing, holding onto other players or dunking the ball or another player underwater. Pass the ball with a soft lob, don't pound it.

STONE TOSS GAMES

A walk along a pebbly beach with a parent or a friend is a relaxing way to end a busy summer's day. You may notice twists of rope, driftwood shapes, bits of animal bone — all weathered remains that have a story to tell.

Here are some objects to pick up on the beach and games to play with them as you walk along.

BULLFROG GLUG

Look for a stone about the size and shape of a plum. It should be heavy and sit easily in the curled palm of your hand.

Check around you. Make sure no one is close by or out in the water. Throw the stone so it arcs high in the air and then falls straight down into the water.

If you make a good throw, and you have a good stone, when it enters the water it will make the glugging sound of a bullfrog croak.

138

S K I P P I N G   S T O N E S

If the water is calm, look along the beach for thin, flat, circular stones, about as a big around as potato chips. Collect a few in your pocket.

Check to make sure no one is in front of you, on either side or in the water. It's okay for friends to stand behind you. Hold a stone so its widest part is held in the U-shaped arc between your index finger and your thumb and its flattest side faces down. Stand so your body is sideways to the water. Bend your knees and hold the stone low, almost level with the water. Swing your arm behind your body and then forward, straightening your index finger as your hand passes your waist.

The stone will run along your finger and then spin toward the water, with the flat side still facing down. When it hits the water surface, it should skip up, fall again, skip up — over and over, until it finally sinks.

How many times can you make it skip? Set a family record, or is that a "rockord"?

FOSSIL WATCH

Some of the stones you pick up may have regular patterns on them, like tiny tire treads or delicate swirls. You may have found a fossil — plant or animal remains from millions of years ago. When the plant or animal died, by chance it was trapped immediately in mud so deep that, over the years, the mud slowly turned to stone. If you find a fossil, you may not want to skip it.

RAFT GAMES

If you are a good swimmer and have a portable raft and life jackets, you can have splashing good fun on a hot day.

RULER OF THE AIR MATTRESS

It's *not* a good idea to swim underwater and tip a friend off a floating air mattress by surprise. In fact, it's both mean and unsafe.

However, you may *agree* to play ruler of the air mattress with a friend; then it can be fair and fun. Both players wear life jackets and swimsuits. Swim the mattress out to chest-deep water, away from rocks, not too far from an adult lifeguard. One player, the ruler, lies on the air mattress. The other swims up from any side and tries to tip the mattress so the ruler flips off or the mattress flips over. The attacker may not touch the lake bottom and neither player may touch the other. If the attacker tips the mattress, the players switch places.

WINDSURFER PIRATES

When it's too calm for windsurfing, find three friends and get permission to use two windsurfing boards. Stow the sails and keels in a safe place. Only the board should remain with no attachments of any kind. Find a sheltered cove to play in, with a watchful adult close by as lifeguard.

- All four players wear swimsuits and life jackets. Players divide into two teams of two.

- On each surfboard, the player at the bow sits up, hands free, and curls her legs and feet under the board to stabilize herself.

- The player at the stern, or rear, lies on his stomach on the board, holding on with his hands and arms. His legs and hips hang off the back to steer and kick the board forward.

- The idea of the game is to take over your opponents' board and not lose control of your own. You can try to flip your opponents off their board. Or you can make the opposing bow person reach so far that she loses her balance and falls off. Whatever you do, you may not ram the other board, hurt the other players or touch the lake bottom.

RAFT RACES

Whether you have air mattresses or inflated inner tubes, you can have wacky raft races. All contestants wear swimsuits and life jackets. Decide on a starting line and finishing line in shoulder-deep water. With an adult as lifeguard, see who can propel her raft to the finish first.

Don't make the course too long. Moving a raft requires a lot of hard kicking and swimming.

DIVING GAMES

If you're a good swimmer, here are some diving games worth holding your breath for. You'll need a safe diving spot where the water is over your head and where you can see the bottom clearly. The deep end of a swimming pool is good or a raft in at least 2.5 m (8 ft.) of water. Ask an adult to check out your diving spot for any hazards, such as jutting rocks, and to act as a lifeguard.

DIVING FOR TREASURE

You can dive for golf balls, clam shells or small painted stones. Toss them into your diving spot. When they fall to the bottom, dive in, open your eyes and see how many you can collect in one breath. Try to increase your speed. Or number the objects with a permanent marker and try to collect them in order.

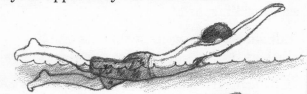

POWER DUCK DIVING

If you have no raft or diving board, you can still search for treasure 2 to 3 m (6 to 9 ft.) down. Learn how to duck dive with power when you are already in the water, swimming forward on your stomach.

1.
Start your duck dive with a hard kick that will lift your upper body out of the water.

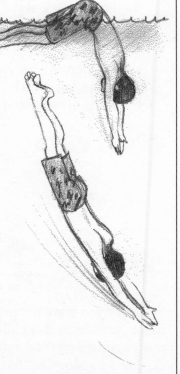

2.
As you kick, stretch your arms ahead, your hands pointed together and your arms touching your ears.

3.
As you finish kicking, bend forward at the waist, point your arms and head down and thrust your bottom up in the air. Keep your legs together, toes pointed, until you are diving straight down. Kick again to add speed to your dive.

CANNONBALL

When you're out of breath from diving for treasure, see who can make the biggest splash.

THE CAN OPENER

Jump farther out, bend and hold one knee as in the cannonball, but keep the other leg outstretched. Hit the water with your bottom and your outstretched leg.

THE REGULAR CANNONBALL

Jump into the water, but before you hit it, bend your knees, tuck your feet up to your bottom and hold your hands together under your knees. The idea is to smack the water with your bottom or knees.

143

BEACH GAMES

Take off your shoes and socks and pull on your favorite hat. Here are more games to play at the beach. Whenever you get too hot, take time out to jump in the water or have a cold drink.

BEACH PADDLEBALL

This game of beach Ping-Pong is played by two people. Each player has a Ping-Pong paddle or a beach paddleball paddle, which is larger. Use a ball that is about the size of a Ping-Pong ball but is very bouncy. It is best to play on hard, damp sand near the water's edge.

Drop the ball and serve it as it falls or when it bounces back up. Aim to hit the sand in front of the other player so the ball can be hit back after one bounce. A sidearm swing may be easiest, but underhand and spike shots are also fair. Have a friendly rally and see how long you can keep the ball going back and forth. Then, try to beat your record. It takes a lot of practice to hit the ball well.

PLAYING THE GAME

You can draw a Ping-Pong-style court in the sand with your heel and play a competitive game. Start with a court about 8 m (25 ft.) long, divided into two 4 m (12½ ft.) ends. The court is for the ball to be shot into — it will bounce well out of the lined area. Players can run outside the lines on their side of the court to return the ball.

1.

The first player serves the ball so it hits the sand in her opponent's half of the court.

2.

The receiving player tries to hit the ball back so it lands on its first bounce in the server's end.

3.

When the server wins the rally, she earns a point.

4.

When the server loses a rally, the serve moves to her opponent, who has a chance to serve and gain points.

5.

Decide before the game whether you will play up to 11 or 15.

MORE

CROCODILE

Did you ever imagine there was a crocodile under your bed, waiting to take a bite out of you when you stepped on the floor? In this game, you pretend that hungry crocodile is lurking in the sand, ready to bite if the beach ball touches the sand.

Lots of people can play. Throw a beach ball in the air and try to keep it moving for as long as possible without hitting the sand. A player cannot hit the ball twice in a row.

The whole group earns one point for every successful hit.

If the ball does hit the beach, the player who last hit the ball is out — eaten by a croc. Try to set a beach record for the number of points earned before the ball hit the sand.

SNAPPING TURTLES, ALLIGATORS AND CROCODILES

Beaches in some parts of the world are closed to people because of the danger of crocodiles or alligators. If you see a 'gator or a croc, find another swimming hole. Even if you come upon a snapping turtle, stand well back. It will probably leave you alone, but it may bite if it feels hungry or threatened.

BEACH VOLLEYBALL

Volleyball is a fast and skilled sport. Here are rules for a not-so-serious outdoor, barefoot version. You'll need a volleyball and two teams of two players each. Sunscreen and a sun hat are a must unless it's raining.

GETTING READY

You'll need a flat area of sand about 18 m x 9 m (60 ft. x 30 ft.) with a volleyball net strung across at the halfway point so the top of the net is about 2.5 m (8 ft.) off the sand. Drag your heel along the sand to mark the outside lines of the court.

bump

volley

spike

underhand serve

marking the court

THE SHOTS

The serve

Release the ball from one hand and punch it over the net with the other.

The volley

Hit the ball with both hands at the same time. The ball is fair if it hits any one part of your body and goes over the net.

The bump

Pass the ball to your partner using your forearm. Bumping is a way to stop a hard shot and set up a volley or spike.

The spike

Jump up and punch the ball to drive it over the net and down into the sand inside your opponent's court. Keep your hands off the net and on your own side of the court.

MORE

PLAYING BEACH VOLLEYBALL

The challenge in beach volleyball is to keep the ball up in the air and moving. You cannot catch, scoop or carry the ball.

1.
The first server stands outside the back line and hits the ball over the net to land inside the opposite court. In a good serve, the ball does not touch the net.

2.
The team receiving the serve can touch the ball three times to get it back over the net. The same player can't hit it twice in a row, unless one hit is a block.

3.
A block happens when a player on one team jumps high and bashes a shot coming over the net back to the other side. In a block, a player's hands can reach over the net into the opponents' side of the court, but should not touch the net. Players from both sides may hit the ball at once.

4.

After a block, if the ball falls on your side of the net, try to hit it up before it touches the sand and get it back over with two more hits.

5.

If the ball strikes the net and bounces back into the same court after the first or second hit, that is okay. If the third hit lands in the net, the side loses.

6.

The rally is over when the ball hits the sand or if a team cannot get the ball over the net in three shots. The winning team serves the next rally.

7.

If the team who just served won, then the same player keeps serving. If the opposing team won, whichever player didn't serve last time takes a turn.

SCORING

The first team to reach 15 points wins. A team has to be serving to score a point. If a team wins a rally when not serving, that team wins the right to serve the next rally and try to score a point.

TIPS

- Use your first two hits to set up a spike. The first hit stops the serve, the second sets up a spike, which is driven home on the third hit.

- Surprise your opponents. Vary your game so that you don't always take three hits to return the ball.

- Use the outdoors to help you win rallies. High shots into the sun are hard to hit back. Gentle shots can be carried by the wind.

CIRCLE SAND GAMES

A damp sandy beach makes a perfect game board. Storage is not a problem, tidying up is a breeze and you never lose the pieces.

WEDGE OF THE WORLD

1.

Draw a circle in the sand the size of a large bicycle tire. Divide the circle into four wedges. Draw a smaller circle in the middle. This is the center of the world.

2.

Find five pieces of driftwood or pebbles of equal size for each player.

3.

Make a line in the sand ten paces away from the circle. The object of the game is to toss a stick or pebble into each of the four large wedges and then land one in the center of the world.

4.

Players take turns, throwing one stick at a time. If the stick lands in a wedge where you already have a stick, or if it lands in the middle before you have a stick in each wedge, you take it back and wait for your next turn.

5.

The first person to place her five sticks correctly is the winner.

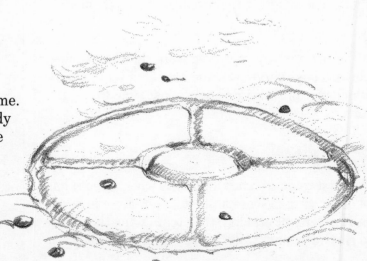

SAND BULL'S-EYE

1.
Draw a circle in the sand the size of a large bicycle tire. Draw a circle in the middle, about the size of a sand pail. Draw two more circles, equal distances apart. From the outside, the rings are worth 1, 2, 3, and the center, 4.

2.
Draw a line in the sand ten paces from the bull's-eye.

3.
Collect three small stones of a similar size.

4.
Players take turns throwing all three stones at the circle. Add up the points scored after each turn. Keep score with pebble counters or a tally in the sand.

5.
The first player to score 50 points is the winner.

DRIP, DRIP, **DROP**

For this game all you need is a sand pail full of water and players wearing swimsuits or play clothes. Add a hot day and a sandy beach and you're all set.

Choose one player to be It. The other players sit in a circle on the sand. It walks slowly around the circle spilling a drip from the pail on each player's head. Everyone says "drip" for each drip. On the head of whichever player he chooses, It dumps out the rest of the water shouting "drop." It drops the pail and runs as fast as he can in one direction around the circle. The wet player jumps up and runs in the opposite direction. The first person back to the empty space sits down. The person left standing is It. Fill the pail and play again.

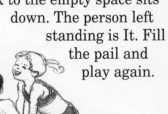

PEBBLES IN THE SAND

Wari is an Egyptian board game that's more than a thousand years old. The game spread to Africa and then traveled with African slaves to America and the West Indies. Wari boards have been dug in the soil or made from wood, stone or pottery. To have your own instant wari board, all you need are 48 small pebbles for counters, a sandy beach and a friend.

GETTING READY

Choose a flat section of beach where the sand is moist, not wet. Scoop out 12 holes about the same depth and distance apart as the holes in an egg carton. This forms the wari board. Place four stones in each hole.

PLAYING THE GAME

1.

Sit on opposite sides of the wari board. The six holes directly in front of each player is her home base. The aim of the game is to capture the counters in your opponent's holes.

2.

Player one picks up four counters from any hole in her row and places or 'sows' one in each of her next four holes to the right (or counterclockwise).

3.

Player two takes a turn as above. Continue taking turns until the last counter sown must go into one of the opponent's holes. If the hole already contains two or three counters, the player captures the counters in that hole, scoops all the counters out and sets them aside. If the hole to the left or right of this hole contains two or three counters, she captures them also.

4.

If there are twelve or more counters in a hole that a player ends in, the player picks up the counters and sows them all the way around the board. Starting with the next hole to the right, she sows one counter per hole, skipping the hole they were removed from.

5.

If the hole contains any number of counters other than two, three or twelve, the new counter is simply added into the hole.

6.

If your opponent's row is empty you must, on your next turn, try to sow at least one counter on her side. If this can't be done, or if a player has no counters left, the game is over and the last person to move gets all the remaining counters on the board. Count them up and the person with the most is the winner.

TIP

As you sow your counters, try to make it impossible for your opponent to land in one of your holes with two or three counters.

PERMANENT WARI

If you want a permanent wari game, use an egg carton as a board. Pebbles, dried beans or shells make good counters. Store your 48 counters inside the egg carton between games.

WARM WEATHER OLYMPICS

At the end of your vacation, take home more than sand between your toes. A well-planned Olympics will guarantee you fantastic memories, new skills and a prize or two. Organize a cooperative and safe event, with everyone from age 2 to 102 taking part. There can be the usual — running races, swimming triathlons, canoe races — and the unusual — an egg toss, watermelon-pit spitting contests and swim-and-sing races. With such fantastic fun, you'll want to be an Olympian every summer.

OLYMPIC PLANNING

Plan and organize your Olympics for maximum success. If you've thought out the day from beginning to end, you will be ready for almost anything. Even the unexpected will be easier when the main events are running smoothly.

GETTING STARTED

- Form a planning committee. Choose one person to be the coordinator. Include one adult as an honorary member of the committee.

- Set a date. Give yourself at least two weeks to get organized.

- Decide how many people you'd like to invite and deliver invitations.

- Choose one committee member to be in charge of prizes. You'll need a trophy for the winning team and a booby prize for the other team. These can be treasures found at garage sales that will be reused every year. Take a trip to the dime store for ribbons, Popsicles and so on, or make your own individual prizes and medals of gold, silver and bronze.

- Invite two or more judges, people who especially suit the job or who can't participate. The judges will keep track of the winners as well as special contributors.

- Set up a lifeguard station, with one adult lifeguard for every eight Olympians. Make sure you have a life ring or a reach pole handy.

SUGGESTED AFTERNOON SCHEDULE

1:30 Participants arrive at Olympic site

1:45 Opening ceremonies

2:00 The games begin

3:00 Snack break

4:00 The grand finale tug-of-war

4:15 Tidy up and prepare for closing ceremonies

4:30 Closing ceremonies

5:00 Banquet

MAKE A MEGAPHONE

Save your voice by making a megaphone for giving instructions. All you need is a file folder or another piece of thin cardboard 30 cm x 40 cm (12 in. x 16 in.), scissors and tape.

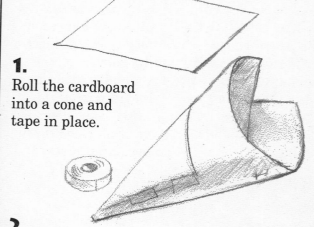

1.
Roll the cardboard into a cone and tape in place.

2.
Trim the narrow end to form a mouthpiece. The hole should be about the size of a dime.

MORE

JUG BUOYS

Make these lane markers before the Olympic day. Set up and test the water challenges with the markers in place. You'll probably need one marker every 3 m (9 ft.). Check your recycling box for large bottles with handles and lids.

You'll need:

clean, empty, plastic bottles with handles and lids

nylon rope

scissors

a heavy rock for each buoy

1.
Peel the labels off the bottles so they don't come off in the water.

2.
Decide where you need water markers.

3.
Measure the depth of the water, using your body as a measuring tape. Cut a piece of rope that will reach the bottom, giving yourself extra rope for tying knots. If the water is too deep, ask an adult to help you measure the length of rope you need.

4.
Attach the rope to the rock at one end and to the handle of a bottle at the other end. Drop the rock in the water at the spot where you need a marker.

CHOOSING EVENTS

The afternoon should include group events for people of all ages, and individual events for athletes divided into age groups such as 4 to 7 years; 8 to 11; 12 to 16; and 16 and over.

For each hour of competition, you'll need between five and seven events. There are many possible events in this book:

500 up, page 12;

horseshoes, page 14;

badminton, page 20;

bootin', page 22;

Frisbee golf, page 26;

21 basketball, page 114;

comet ball, page 116;

water polo, page 136;

diving, page 142;

Ping-Pong, page 144

beach volleyball, page 147.

Round out the list of events with some Land and Water challenges (pages 160–169) and your own ideas.

OPENING CEREMONIES

When everyone has assembled, divide into two teams. Each team selects a leader. The coordinator welcomes everyone, briefly explains the events and reminds everyone of the safety rules.

WATER CHALLENGES

On your mark, get set, wait! Check out swimming and diving safety on page 132 before you begin. Then try for a record, cheer on the team, and have a safe and fun-filled afternoon.

GETTING READY

Set up for any water events with the help of an adult. The beach area should be clean, and the water free from sharp objects, tied-up boats or underwater surprises. Use natural landmarks or stationary objects — the point, the sandbar, the dock, the raft — to define the water area. Jug buoys (see page 158) can mark swimming or boating lanes, starting and finishing lines and boundaries so that they are clear to everyone.

SWIMMING EVENT TIPS

- Involve all ages and skill levels with a variety of swim challenges.

- Before the races start, divide the group into swimmers and nonswimmers. All nonswimmers must wear life jackets.

- Avoid diving accidents. Start all races in the water, not from the shore or dock.

- Ask a nonswimmer to be the official starter. She can use the megaphone.

- Ask the judges to pick the top three competitors in each event. Everyone should encourage and cheer on all participants.

160

SWIMMING RACES

KNEE-HIGHS

Short, freestyle race for 2 to 4 year olds in life jackets. All participants should get a prize.

CONVENTIONAL STROKES

Individual races of front crawl, breaststroke, sidestroke, backstroke and butterfly, divided by age group.

LONG DISTANCE

Freestyle race following a predetermined course for good swimmers only, divided by age group. Adult supervision is required, and a small boat equipped with life jackets and a reach pole should escort the swimmers.

UNUSUAL SWIMMING RACES

SHALLOW-WATER CHALLENGE

Bob or handstand a required number of times from start to finish.

SHORT DISTANCE

Duck dive (see page 142) continuously from start to finish.

MULTISTROKE MEDLEY

One length of front crawl, one of
sidestroke, one of breaststroke,
one of backstroke.

MINI-MARATHON

Front crawl from the dock to the rock, sidestroke from the rock to the buoy,
breaststroke from the buoy to the point, backstroke to the finish line.

SING AND SWIM

Swim, with your head out of the water,
while singing the national anthem. If you
stop singing, you have to start over.

WATERMELON DASH

Run one length in waist-deep
water, carrying a watermelon.

FIND THE FLOATERS

Throw a pail full of corks or
Ping-Pong balls into the swimming
area. At the count of three, all swimmers
from both teams retrieve the corks and place
them in two piles on the shore or dock. The
team that collects the most corks wins.

MORE

161

R E L A Y S

Churn up the water and get your heart racing with a rousing relay. Divide the participants by team or by age group.

Each swimmer completes two lengths of the swimming area. Swimmer one does the breaststroke; swimmer two, the sidestroke; swimmer three, the backstroke; swimmer four, the front crawl. If there are more than four swimmers, repeat the strokes in order. Each swimmer must tag the next swimmer or pass on a diving ring.

CRAZY R E L A Y S

Turn tradition on its ear and make your Olympics extra fun with crazy relays. Try some of these combinations and add some of your own. Look through the boathouse to find as many props as possible. Incorporate them into your relays. List the relays you want to include on a poster tacked up near the starting line.

- Swimmer one puts a flutterboard under his feet and swims one length, arms only, on his back.

- Swimmer two puts an old swimsuit on over her suit and swims one length singing "Boom Boom, Ain't It Great To Be Crazy."

- Swimmer three holds an air mattress under one arm and swims one length.

- Swimmer four swims one length carrying a boat bumper.

- Swimmer five sits on an inflated toy and paddles one length backward with her hands.

- Swimmer six swims one length pushing a water balloon with her nose.

BOAT RACES

Sailing, windsurfing and canoeing events are perfect for a regatta. Set up a course of local landmarks (to the point, the buoy, the neighbors' dock) for the boats to travel to and around. If there aren't many boats available, participants can take turns and record their times. Don't forget to include a crazy boat relay: carry the boat from up on the shore down to the water, put on a baseball cap sideways, paddle out to the raft using arms as paddles, make a T-shirt sail and sail to the dock, eat five crackers and whistle a song, and whatever else you can dream up.

GOOSE BUMPS

If you are in and out of the water a lot, you may get cold. As air moves across your skin, the water evaporates, which cools you down. You may even shiver or get goose bumps. Shivering helps warm you up. And although goose bumps are an ancient, natural way to warm up your body too, they don't work anymore.

The earliest humans were different from us because they had hair all over their bodies. When those people got cold, tiny muscles in their skin tensed up to make that hair puff up and hold warm air next to their bodies. Our skin still makes goose bumps when we get cold. But it's been many millennia since we had enough hair to hold in our body heat.

If you get goose bumps or shiver, you're losing body heat quickly. Find a dry towel or clothes and dry yourself off. Cover your head if your hair is wet. Cooling down is okay, but losing too much body heat is dangerous!

BEACH BIATHLON

In the Winter Olympics, the biathlon is an event that mixes the endurance of cross-country skiing with target challenges. You can create your own crazy, summer biathlon on the beach and see who can finish in the shortest time.

GETTING READY

Look for a selection of balls: golf balls, beach balls, tennis balls, softballs, soccer balls, Ping-Pong balls, red rubber balls. With the owners' permission, collect old "sticks" too: hockey sticks, ax handles, oars, croquet mallets, paddles, golf clubs, tennis rackets, spoons, badminton rackets, broom handles, baseball bats. Each contestant gets to choose a ball and a stick.

Lay out a biathlon course about 300 paces long. On the beach, drag your heel or a stick to mark the course. Leave pebble markers to indicate the route on grassy or rough terrain.

At the 100 and 200 pace points, set up target stations. At one station, you could leave slices of watermelon and instructions that each contestant eat one slice and spit five pits at least 2 m (6 ft.). The other station might have three Ping-Pong balls and instructions to throw them into flowerpots about 1 m (3 ft.) away. Or you can think up your own target challenges.

During the event, you'll need helpers: a starter, a timer and two target judges.

THE EVENT

Contestants leave from the starting line every 30 seconds. They tap or dribble their balls along the course with their sticks, stop to complete each target challenge, and then dribble over the finishing line. The winner is the one who finishes first, having successfully met the target challenges.

LAND CHALLENGES

Turn from the water and beach to dry land for more individual and team competitions. Tell participants to wear a sun hat, sunscreen and a swimsuit or clothes that can get dirty.

For most events you'll need a starting and finishing line, a person to start the race and someone to judge the winner.

R A C E S

Divide competitors into age groups to keep the races fair. Or, vary the finishing line so smaller kids have shorter distances to cover from the same starting line. Organize traditional events like the 100 m (100 yd.) dash, cross-country run and bike races. But don't stop there — try some crazy race events too:

BACKWARD RACE

Contestants run backward, but are allowed to twist their head so they can see where they are going.

CRAB RACE

Contestants place their hands on the ground behind them and, with only hands and feet touching the ground, race forward, backward or sideways to the finish line.

SACK RACE

Hop from start to finish standing in a big bag, holding the top edge of the bag with your hands. Use burlap or sturdy plastic bags from the local feed mill, garden center or bulk grocery store.

WHEELBARROW RACE

A partnered race in which one person runs behind, holding the hind feet of the other who moves forward on her hands.

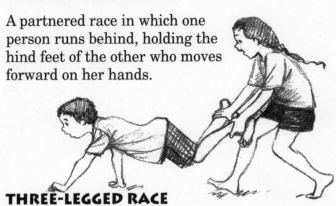

THREE-LEGGED RACE

Two people run side by side with one leg tied to their partner's at the ankle.

BIG SHOUT RACE

The winner runs the farthest, shouting the whole time. This is an endurance race, contestants drop out when they have no more lung power to shout.

THROWING EVENTS

No Olympics is complete without throwing events. Who can throw a baseball the farthest? Add a few wacky throwing events such as:

A FEATHER THROW

Who can throw a feather into the wind, the farthest?

AN EGG TOSS

Partners throw a raw egg back and forth. Every time they are successful, they each take a giant step backward and try again. Which pair can toss the egg the farthest without it breaking?

A BALLOON HISS

Who can blow up a balloon and let it go farthest, propelled by its own escaping air?

167

LAND R E L A Y S

Add more fun to your homestyle Olympics with relays on high, dry ground. The relay can start and finish at the same point with each member racing to the turnaround point and back to tag the next member. Or a land relay can be spread along a long course with team members at various points down the way waiting for their turn. Participants are divided into teams of four or more.

Here are some wacky relay ideas to mix and match with traditional running relays. After completing your stint, don't forget to run on and tag the next team member!

WET T-SHIRT RELAY

Run to a pail of water, take out a wet T-shirt, put it on right over your clothes, do a dance, take it off, put it back in the pail.

MARSHMALLOW RELAY

Run to a bench where marshmallows are pressed against ice cubes so they stick. Choose one, chew the marshmallow off the ice cube with your hands behind your back.

BALLOON-BREAK RELAY

Run to a chair, blow up a balloon, put it on the chair, sit on the balloon until it breaks.

BANANA RELAY

Run a distance with a banana between your knees, pass the banana to the next member of your team to carry in some crazy way. That person then passes it on and when the last member crosses the finishing line, everyone on the team sits down, breaks up the banana and eats it. The winning team is the first to whistle a tune.

OLDSTYLE OLYMPICS

Although we model our modern Olympics on the ancient games, some of the most ancient events would *not* fit well into your land challenges.

- In 776 B.C. at the very first Olympics, the only event was the stade, a sprint from one end of the stadium to the other. The athletes were all men who wore no clothes and smeared their bodies with oil.

- The two-, four- and eight-stade races were added later. Players were allowed to elbow and push at the turning posts.

- By Roman times, the most popular event was the pancratium: a fight between two men that allowed biting, kicking, eye-gouging and strangling to death.

COOPERATIVE GAMES

Get the whole gang working together for a change. Set up a challenge that will not be successful unless everyone helps one another to complete it.

◆ ◆ ◆ ◆ ◆ ◆ ◆ ◆ ◆ ◆ ◆ ◆ ◆

LIFE RAFT

This game is played on land, but you pretend the ground is shark-infested water. For a group of ten, you'll need a beach towel. If you have more friends who want to join in, grab an old tablecloth or sheet.

PLAYING THE GAME

1.
Lay the towel flat on the ground.

2.
Challenge your friends to huddle on the cloth so that no one touches the ground beyond. Hold that position for a count of ten.

3.
When you've accomplished that feat, fold the towel in half and try again.

4.
See how small a space you can all huddle on — with no one getting a toe nibbled off by the circling sharks.

S P I D E R   W E B

1.

Find a place where two trees grow about 3 m (9 ft.) apart. Take a full ball of nylon rope and tie one end to one tree, about 30 cm (1 ft.) up the trunk. Pull the rope up the side of the tree, and loop it around the same trunk and knot it again at 1 m (3 ft.) and 2 m (6 ft.) for strength.

2.

Pull the rope across to the other tree, loop and tie around that trunk at about 2 m (6 ft.), 1 m (3 ft.) and 30 cm (1 ft.) too. Complete the rectangle by returning the rope to the first knot.

3.

Now, weave a web between the two trees. Leave some spaces about 65 cm (2 ft.) square in the mesh. If you have any little decorative bells on threads or elastics, dangle them onto some of the strands of the web.

4.

Challenge the whole group to get through the web without touching the strands or trees so as not to awaken the people-eating spider. Only one person in the group is allowed to crawl under the web.

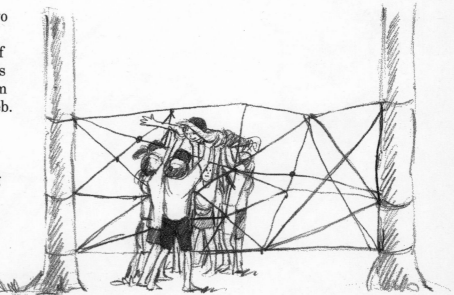

THE GRAND FINALE

One last contest and then on to the party.

The ultimate test of muscle power and skill is a tug-of war — the only event in which both teams work together at the same time. May yours be the lucky team that stays clean and dry.

TUG-OF-WAR

1.
You'll need a strong piece of rope, no less than 20 m (60 ft.) in length. Mark the middle of the rope with a ribbon or bandanna.

2.
Find the right tug site on a beach, lawn or field. Choose a spot where both teams will have similar footing and lay the rope flat on the ground. Mark a line on the ground under the ribbon, or place the middle of the rope over marsh, mud or a puddle.

3.
The teams should have an equal number of participants. Ask an extra person to be the referee.

TIPS

- The team leader can watch the other team and yell, "Pull!" Try to catch the other team off guard.

- The anchor should dig in his heels.

CLOSING CEREMONIES

Plan a time to tally up the afternoon's efforts. The coordinator of the Warm Weather Olympics should act as the master of ceremonies, make a speech, help give out prizes and thank everyone.

Make sure to recognize the accomplishments of all participants and not just the person who swam the fastest front crawl. Award a crazy prize to the Olympian who:

- soaked the most towels
- had the most goose bumps
- was the most enthusiastic
- drank the most lake water
- ate the most watermelon
- made the most noise
- splashed the most water

When the speeches are over, dig into a potluck banquet. Everyone will probably be starved.

4.
The team leader arranges her team along the rope. She will be the first in line, 3 m (9 ft.) from the middle ribbon. The last person is called the anchor. He should be the biggest and strongest person on the team. The anchor holds the rope 1 m (3 ft.) from the end.

5.
When both teams are all set, the referee shouts, "Go." The object of the game is to pull the rope and the opposing team until the leader has been pulled over the line.

INDEX